Simplify and Organize: Effortless Tips for Decluttering Your Home

Alexander B. Sanchez

How to Declutter Your Home

Many people find the concept of living a simple life with less belongings appealing.

However, people frequently get overwhelmed, scared, and defeated by the prospect of possessing less. That's unfortunate.

Learning how to declutter your house (and, by extension, your life) does not have to be as difficult as some make it out to be. And the advantages are numerous.

The Advantages of Life Decluttering
There are several advantages to having less stuff. Even yet, taking action is difficult. That is, until the numerous advantages of decluttering become apparent:

There is less to clean. Cleaning is obviously a hassle, but having to clean around objects you have no emotional affinity to (or, worse, genuinely despise) makes it even more difficult.

There is less to arrange. Finding stuff becomes much easier. Things do not just "vanish" any longer. Instead of navigating around objects that are in the way, you may move around your home and appreciate the space.

Debt reduction. Spending less time shopping for material stuff and adding to the clutter keeps your wallet and bank accounts larger, your credit card balances lower, and your house free of expensive items you don't need.

More financial independence. According to a recent Charles Schwab poll conducted in May 2019, the majority of American households live paycheck to paycheck (59%). Almost half of those polled have credit card debt. Decluttering, in conjunction with minimalism, will assist you in accumulating money to protect yourself in the event of an unforeseen need.

More vitality for your most ardent interests. With less debt, greater financial independence, and a clean house, you can now devote your time and energy to activities that you like rather than worrying about "keeping up with the Joneses." This will eventually make you happy.

So you've learned the advantages of decluttering your life, but you might be stumped by the following question... Where on earth do you begin?

Making a checklist is one of the simplest methods to keep track of what may and must be removed from your house. We've created a Declutter Your Home Checklist that you may use to make an immediate difference.

Certainly not. You can get rid of the clutter in your home on your own. When applying the decluttering techniques in this article, it may even be an enjoyable family activity.

Clutter removal from our homes and lives does not have to be rushed or completed in a single day. It's something that can be done gradually and may even be necessary on a semi-regular basis. If you begin the process today, you will be further along than you were yesterday.

CONTENTS

Chapter One: My Home Is Messy, I Wonder Why! 1
Chapter Two: C'Mon, Get Rid of 'Em! 35
Chapter Three: Organizing by Genre 77
Chapter Four: Now Let's Organize What Is Left, Or "What You Really Love!" 124
Chapter Five: Declutter Your Life! 168

CHAPTER ONE: MY HOME IS MESSY, I WONDER WHY!

Unless you've grown up under parents or guardians that were fastidious in how tidy they were, have been put through military training, or have a knack for liking things clean to begin with, decluttering isn't something that comes so easily to everyone. Life can become hectic, and when one aspect of our lives (aside from our homes) becomes messy, so too does that reflect in the place we live. One thing leads to another, and before you know it you have not only wall-to-wall furniture but floor-to-ceiling and everywhere-you-step piles of objects that once sounded like a great deal to have! Think back to how you got into your situation where the clutter-bug really bit you. Did it start with a can't-miss sale at the department store? A stress-buy at the furniture lot? Or maybe even you went antiquing, found a lost treasure of Versailles, and now you don't know where to put it because it doesn't match the rest of your decor?

If this sounds like you then first of all congratulations on your discovery for some admittedly really cool objects, and second of all it's time to get your shit together. If you walk into every store with the mindset of getting every deal on the shelf, then I hate to break it to you, but that's an unsustainable lifestyle that will cause your detriment when it comes to your home. There's nothing wrong with treating yourself by getting something you really want so long as you have the room. Ask yourself when grabbing the adorable throw pillow you find; "how many of these do I have at home?" When swiping up a new purse because it's gorgeous and half off, recall how many you have in your closet. Do you use them every single time you go out, or do you just have a pile sitting around that you found by doing the same thing before?

It's not just material possessions that have this issue, but for those of us who are often too tired or encumbered by the doldrums of work, coming home to order a pizza or takeout is so much easier than cooking. Unless you tidy up right away, you could be prone to leaving bigger messes behind that could attract all manner of vermin. The last thing you want is a mouse living in your old pizza boxes, as cute as they can sometimes be. This goes as well for the dishes in the sink, new kitchen gadgets, and so forth.

Let's give the benefit of the doubt though, maybe you're not a shopaholic or prone to reach for the phone when hungry but have many excessively generous people that care about you. They seem to be giving you a new set of china plates every time you visit, or a piece of furniture they don't want, maybe even sending you home with so much food that your fridge can't fit it all anymore. The point is that clutter comes in many different forms, and however you've begun your overaccumulation of items around your home there are ways to mitigate the issue at its root cause.

The first step in really beginning your journey on cleaning up the mess you made is changing your mindset. In order to begin, you have to tell yourself "no." No, you do not need another set of plates. No, you don't want another stack of pizza boxes in your house. No, you don't need a new purse. Sometimes, self-care begins with the word "no," and you should never feel guilty turning down an offer. I won't pretend this is easy, occasionally when I have to insist on declining a kind gesture I can really feel like the bad guy. However, when being mindful of your situation, you have to act purely in your own interest (at least to begin with). This will take a lot of discipline, practice, and self-checking, but over time it will become easier to be more mindful of what you take home. Your cluttered home is, after all, what got you reading this far. Once you've decided to stop adding to your mess, you can genuinely begin the process of decluttering.

In the following first exercise , take the time to identify any bad habits you may have when it comes to collecting objects in your home. How do you think it got to this point? Take your time and come back to this if you would like to once you've given it a bit more thought!

EXERCISE# 1
HELLO, I HAVE A BAD HABIT!

Date: ---------

Below, you can pick out bad habits you've made when it comes to bringing things home. What's something you have trouble saying no to? What got you where you are? Let's start out journey with a little self reflection!

"Do you want to know who you are? Don't ask.

Act! Action will delineate and define you."

Thomas Jefferson

Beginning the Journey of Decluttering

To begin, first, understand that you may be unaccustomed to trying to take care of their spaces and might not be sure where to start. There's plenty of information about how to do so, found with a simple web search. However, a lot of the advice given by strangers online is, unsurprisingly, not too helpful. Based on my own research with different seminars and studies I've read about, there are quite a few articles that tell you to try cleaning up your mess one day at a time. By picking one thing and putting it away, eventually, the clutter will go away. I am here to tell you that I've tried that, and it absolutely does not work. By picking up a little every day, you are also still contributing to your own clutter because you still live and work in the space you're struggling to tidy. Would you use a toothpick to dig a hole in the soil when you could instead be using a shovel? This is a common mistake when it comes to cleaning since it's a solution suggested by several people across various websites. Stick with me, however, and I'll tell you what you should be doing instead.

Imagine during a hot summer you're stuck driving through a construction zone with a lane packed full of cars. Your air conditioner broke earlier today, and you're drenched in sweat, making you tired and more irritable as time goes by. It takes two hours to get through this area, and then when you finally pass by the workers, you glance over to see they've decided not to use a bulldozer but instead a couple of household spoons to clear away what they need to. You'd be frustrated just looking at them! This same concept should apply to cleaning; why should you pick away at anything in an insufficient way when you have the tools already available to get the job done as quickly as possible? If you're flustered by the rate at which construction workers move on the side of the road; remember that's exactly what your life looks like inside your home.

Have you come across a situation that's made you frustrated by the speed at which it was completed? Write down the first thing that comes to mind when you think of an incident that's ever made you impatient. How would you have fixed the situation from the end of those causing you to hold up?

Fun Exercise #2 - Digging with Spoons

Check out the second exercise, take your time as each one prepares you to the following step.

EXERCISE# 2
DIGGING WITH SPOONS

Date: ---------

In the past, I've been through a tough situation in which

However, I managed to fix it by

"Dream your own dreams,
Achieve your own goals.
Your journey is your own and unique."

Roy T. Bennett

Self Reflection 1

Use the space below to begin journaling your thoughts. Many more sections will appear just like this one as we proceed. Make use of them, as they'll be important for your "declutter therapy!"

When it comes to planning how you're going to proceed with cluttering your home, shoot for idealism. Don't go slowly, instead aim to get everything done all at once so you don't have to come home to a messy home ever again—at least, not to the extent it's gotten. Continually living in a mess will only have you proceed to live in depression or at the very least irritability. By committing to taking care of everything right away, you'll be able to rip off the band aid of discourse sewn into one of the most important places of your life; your very home. A cluttered space is a cluttered mind; once your base of operations is in order, you'll find everything else in your life falls right into place.

Start thinking about it! Is there a specific room you're just itching to see the floor in again? Try brainstorming how you might begin and in what room you'll get started. Don't begin cleaning up just yet, though! There are still some things we must go over. Instead, use the exercise below to start brainstorming ideas and visualizing what it'll be like to have an organized space again.

Fun Exercise #3 - Choosing Your Starting Point

This one is Really a Fun one!

EXERCISE# 3
CHOOSING YOUR STARTING POINT

Date: ---------

Let's visualize how the rooms in your home will look like once decluttered and organized (close your eyes and visualize for at least five minutes, try to be as detailed as possible on how your dream home would be).

Then, create a list of the order you want to start your decluttering journey through your home, the exercise includes space for living room, bedroom, kitchen, bathroom etc.

Please refer to the complete exercise# 3 in your booklet "download it from the "free gift" section at the beginning of the book), here's how the exercise look like

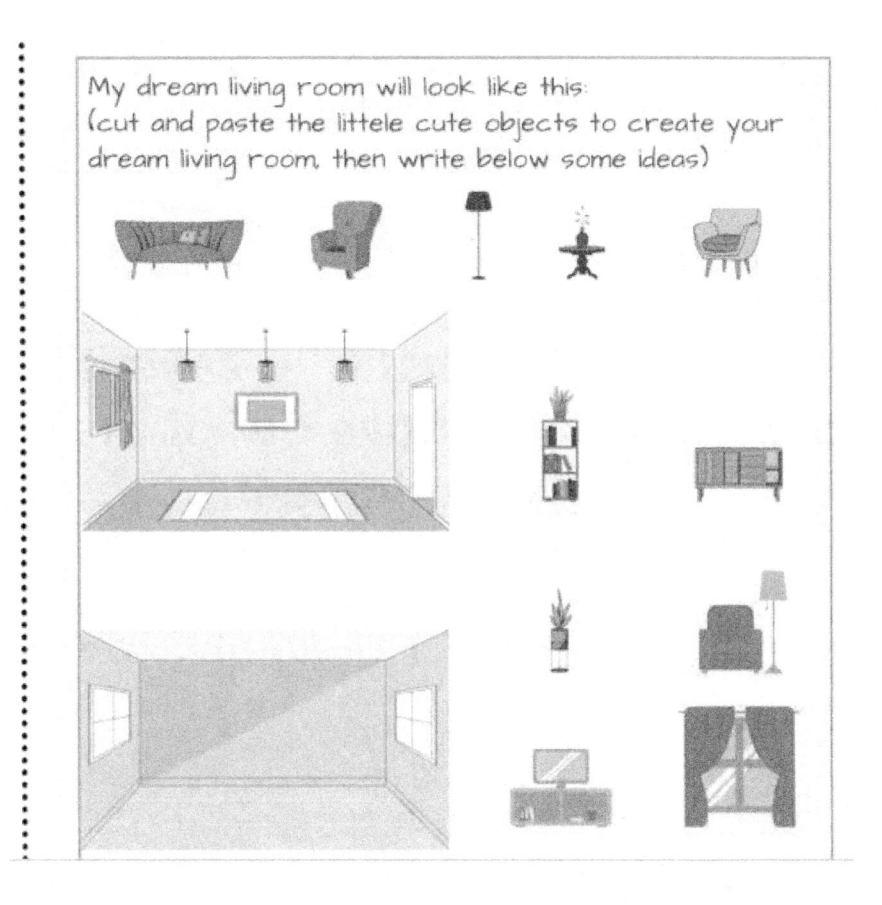

My dream living room will look like this:
(cut and paste the littele cute objects to create your dream living room, then write below some ideas)

"The individual who says it is not possible should move out of the way of those doing it."

Tricia Cunningham

Avoid the Lure of "Saving It for Later"

This is another common problem when it comes to those of us who have a lot of items in our homes. Rather than deciding to get rid of things for good, you come up with the idea that maybe, just maybe, you could put away the things you like, but still own them. You want your cake and you'll eat it too! This would lead to renting out a storage facility you pay for monthly, or keeping things with a friend, your parents' basement, anywhere but your home. DO NOT DO THIS! By mashing together all the things you *may* want later, you are not taking care of the problem but instead sweeping it under the rug to be handled at a later day. All the possessions you love piled away in (let's assume) a storage closet, until over time you forget what's inside completely. It's as if you've taken all your peas and carrots, overheated them in the microwave, and mashed them up so much that you can't even distinguish what's what anymore. This is something I like to call "Storage Mush."

Storage mush is one of the worst things you could possibly do to sabotage yourself on the road to improving your way of life. You do not deal with the problem, and so even after the clutter is no longer in your home, you'll continue to fill your home with the same amount of items again, which could lead to a cycle of purchasing storage units. Atop all the mental problems that arose when you first found your home too messy to bear, now your wallet is sinking too. Monthly payments come out to pay for the unit, and in the end, all you've done is add more to your problems. Doing something like this is the equivalent of slapping a Hello Kitty band aid onto an open, gaping wound. **Instead, you absolutely must commit to the idea that you will have to get rid of some of the things you currently own.**

Do you currently rent any storage facilities or use a loved one's space to store your things? If so, do you remember what all is inside it, and do you need any of it anymore? If you don't have anything in storage, then is there anything in your home you haven't used in a long time? Use the exercise below to begin organizing your thoughts on things you might not have a use for anymore!

Fun Exercise #4 - Do I *Really* Need It?

EXERCISE# 4
CHOOSING YOUR STARTING POINT

Date: ---------

Do I really need it?

I don't really use those anymore, I don't even like them:

"The foolish man seeks happiness in the distance.

The wise grow it under his feet."

James Oppenheim

Self Reflection 2

Now that we're getting started, what are your thoughts? Are you anxious about decluttering your house? Are you excited? There's a lot that's about to happen, so take a moment to jot down what you're thinking about.

Declutter by Genre, Not by Location

When getting started, it's easy to begin picking up a room. The problem is *staying* in that room. Let me explain with another example. Let's say you've chosen the living room to start picking up in. Among the first few objects you touch are the TV remote, your hairbrush, a few stacks of magazines, and an old water cup. You start by organizing the stack of magazines, throwing out the old ones. You place the remote onto the coffee table. Then, you put the hairbrush and the water cup on the end table by the couch. Already, you've done something wrong.

First of all, it's a great idea to put the remote and (newer) magazines on your coffee table where you'll find them, but there's no reason the old water cup and your hairbrush need to stay in the living room. The hairbrush should go in a designated drawer of your bathroom and the water cup to the sink in preparation to be washed. This seems like an obvious concept but just think of your current living room. Are there children's toys laying all around, loose change on the bottom of jars, old decorations you have yet to take down? Small objects have a habit of "walking away" from where they're supposed to be, especially when life gets really busy. Just because you started tidying up in this area doesn't mean you or the items you pick up are bound to it with a ball and chain. This is one of the most powerful secrets when thinking about how to start decluttering your home.

Instead of focusing on the space in which you begin to clean, think instead about where each item belongs, then go room by room! Think of it this way, you start in the living room again but this time you ONLY have items in mind that would go to the bathroom. Then you go around the house, room by room, making necessary stops to the bathroom to drop off the items once your arms are full, rinse and repeat until everything is where it should be. This is a great way to get started cleaning up your home, and it's something that can be done in no time at all. Make different trips around the house with different genres in mind. "What belongs in my bedroom? What belongs in my kitchen?" This "Genre Method" is something we'll come back to again and again over the course of this workbook.

BONUS: If you toss away items you didn't really end up needing as you do the genre method, that's even better! The more you do this, the easier it will become to throw away objects you once thought you desperately needed. When going around your house, keep a garbage bag in your hand. This way you can throw away items you no longer want or need into the bin. Talk about killing two birds with one stone! Otherwise, make a pile of things that you want to be donated in an area that will keep the items out of the way while you work. You can sort through this pile later as you get ready to move it for transport.

Fun Exercise #5 - A New Genre

Let's try this out right now! Think of your bedroom and walk around your house. As you do, use the chart below to write down what items you pick up and where you found them. You might be surprised where some of these objects that usually belong in your room ended up!

EXERCISE# 5
A NEW GENRE

Date: ---------

Please refer to the complete exercise# 5 in your booklet, as you will find spaces for all rooms.

In my living room I found:

And I:

- Threw it away
- Returned it to its home
- Donated it

In my bedroom I found:

And I:

- Threw it away
- Returned it to its home
- Donated it

And so on.

"Don't let mental blocks control you. Set yourself free. Confront your fear and turn the mental blocks into building blocks."

— Dr Roopleen

Change Your Mind(set)

Perhaps one of the most difficult things to overcome when starting out on a goal for a tidier household is the idea that what you're about to do is work and lots of it. This attitude is deadly to your outset, and if every single move you make to get closer to your finish line comes with groaning, whining, or even procrastination then you will be that much worse off. Think of decluttering not as a chore, but as an occasion to be celebrated. If you use this book correctly and follow all the ideas, concepts, and instructions you'll find that major decluttering like this won't become an everyday occurrence, but a once or twice a year event that you can turn into a holiday of sorts. Rather than thinking of everything you're about to do by organizing your life as a chore, make it fun! Plan one or two days of nothing but focusing on your mess, commit to not cooking anything in that time to not add more dishes or clutter to your piles. In these moments, reaching for the phone is acceptable for ordering a pizza, or planning ahead to store some sandwiches in your fridge. Since this is a "holiday" event of cleaning, maybe order out from a restaurant. By making little changes to the course of your day, you'll find it'll become so much easier to get through! Another way to help you along as you get going is to make a game out of it. See how much you can declutter in the span of ten minutes. Then, try to beat your record. You can find plenty of ways to make decluttering that much more enjoyable.

Fun Exercise #6 - Speed Cleaning

Let's try this out! Pick a genre to stick with for the time being and attempt to pick up or put away as many things as possible in a set time limit. This can be thirty minutes, an hour, or anything you choose. Then keep score and see if you can't beat it the next round!

EXERCISE# 6
SPEED CLEANING

Date: ---------

I will choose the --------------genre,

In 10 minutes, I collected ---- items   Date:

In --- minutes; I collected ---- items   Date:

In --- minutes; I collected ---- items   Date:

In --- minutes; I collected ---- items   Date:

In --- minutes; I collected ---- items   Date:

In --- minutes; I collected ---- items   Date:

Repeat it for other genres.

"To progress in life, I don't focus on how much I have done but how much I have yet to do".

Idowu Koyenikan

By choosing to declutter your home with the right attitude, you'll find your work goes by much smoother than if you didn't. If trying to make it a special occasion by adjusting the events of the day still doesn't help you feel better about it then suck it up, buttercup! The truth is that you're going to continue feeling negative about yourself and the space you live in so long as it looks like a homeless camp. Try to envision how much better you'll feel when your air doesn't smell like week-old cheese in a hot car; Let that be the motivation you need to roll up your sleeves and get to work. Remember that you're only going to need to do this *once or twice a year* if you do this right, so commit to it and see it through. Giving up halfway is not an option if you want to improve your current livelihood.

Self Reflection 3

Keeping a home free of clutter is a battle of wits against yourself. It's very easy to sabotage ourselves by "accepting" that human nature can't be helped. What do you think? How did you get to this point in your life? Were you raised in a messy household, or do you consider yourself to be a bit lazy?

It's Not My Fault, I Was Just Born Messy!

This is something I've heard often when consulting with friends and family about their own clutter. In fact, it's exactly what I thought of myself before I became the "Guru of Cleanliness" among my peers. I suffered from the idea that because I had always been fairly untidy, that there would be no point in trying. That I was stuck in an endless cycle of trash in my home, which made me feel like trash in return. Now that I've taken the time to better myself through academic study, extensive research, and countless hours of practice, here's exactly what I think about that kind of mindset: BULLSHIT! The truth is either no one helped you when you really needed a better understanding of your own ability to hold yourself accountable for your space, or you or a family suffered from depression which made you immobile in cases of self-care. There could be dozens of reasons why you feel that you're incapable of picking yourself up to take care of your home, but I'm here to tell you that those are just excuses you tell yourself to procrastinate. The truth is that you are a wonderful, capable, unique person that can do *anything* you set your mind to. If I could make the change to improve myself, then you can too.

Here's what we're going to do; we're going to make you feel more confident so that you know that you're not cursed to a life living side-by-side with the DVD collection you keep meaning to put away. If you feel that you are "born messy," then you first need to prove to yourself above all others that that is wrong. It's a mean thought to have about yourself, and incredibly reductive to your means of self-improvement. By pigeon-holing yourself to the title of "messy," you may feel like you're naturally just going to make your home a cluttered mess again despite your best efforts. I promise you, that's not going to happen. Anyone, anywhere, can improve themselves overnight if they just put their mind to it. That is exactly what you're going to do, so get ready for your overnight "makeover." The new you is gonna be tidy, observant of your surroundings, and prepared to tackle any challenge when it comes to keeping your home, and thus your life, in order!

Fun Exercise #7 - Shut the Hell Up!

Let's build that confidence up! Positive affirmations are a great way to get yourself motivated and enthusiastic for taking care of yourself and your home. Try finding three things you love about yourself, then writing those individual things down each time. For example: "I love my ability to wake up in the morning and make myself my favourite blend of coffee before work." By being kind to yourself, you'll find you'll be able to improve your mood right away and put yourself in the mindset you need to take care of your mess! "Born-Messy-Be-Gone!"

EXERCISE# 7
SHUT THE HELL UP!

Date: ---------

Self-affirmation encourages you to think positively about the important things in your life.

Some examples of affirmations that you can use daily:

- I create a safe and secure space for myself wherever I am.
- I am confident in my ability to ---------------
- I accept my emotions and let them serve their purpose.

Create your own personalized affirmations below:

"The time and effort you sacrifice now is a seed you plant to harvest later on".

Jakson Taviri

Self Reflection 4

Use this section to freely write your thoughts and feelings about your current state of living. Nothing is too much or too little to job down. Decluttering your mind is just as important as decluttering your surroundings.

CHAPTER TWO: C'MON, GET RID OF 'EM!

Alright, you've had some practice and worked through your misgivings, so the time for handholding is over! This is where the real work begins, and it starts with throwing out all the crap you got on sale and haven't touched in over a year. Your goal as of right now is going to be throwing out all the shit you don't need as quickly as you can. Like ripping off a Band-Aid—no delays, no worries, no more putzing around. If you hold off on this step or hesitate, you could make the mistake of overthinking it and as a result, keeping things you don't need. This way you'll feel the difference on the spot, your mood instantly lifting the moment all that crap is out the door! Right now, don't even worry about organization. All you need to focus on is "what do I get rid of?"

It can be admittedly difficult to come up with exactly what should be tossed or kept, so a good rule of thumb to follow is by asking yourself this question when you pick something up. "Have I used this or needed this in the past single year?" If the answer is no, chuck it! The only kind of organizing you should be doing is figuring out what to donate, what to sell, what to recycle, and what to put in the trash bin. If you're going to sell something, take it somewhere out of sight where you can't see it before putting it up for sale on whichever website you prefer. That way it's out of the way and, in your mind, already gone. This can also be accomplished with a yard sale, but regardless, it's gotta go!

A good place to start is your closet. An overabundance of clothing is a common issue, and for those who are prone to keeping your clutter on hand, it can be hard to get rid of! Ask yourself as you go through each individual item, "Have I worn this in the last year?

Does this have holes in it? Is this important to me for any sentimental reason?" If you haven't worn it in a year, or the cloth has become home to moths, and it's not sentimental, GET RID OF IT!!

On a softer note, let me say that sometimes we as humans want to hold onto things that are bad for us. This could be mementos of a sad time, or a time of mourning, or a time where you were in a very tough space. It is tempting to hold onto a horrible past, but your memories are your momentos. Remove the pieces—the proof of your life that shows these days gone by. If you have ever suffered from trauma and kept items from that time; throwing it away or even destroying it completely in your way of choice could be the first step to your therapeutic breakthrough. The people or things that hurt you once do not deserve a place in your life, your heart, your mind, and most definitely not your home. I have been hurt, and in my journey to decluttering my life, I also had to throw these momentos away.

Here is a tasteful list of things you could say as you throw away or destroy these relics of pain:

- Good (BLEEP)ing Riddance
- Get the (BLEEP) out of my life
- You don't own me anymore, (BLEEP)hole
- You never (BLEEP)ing deserved me
- I hope you burn like this (object you're destroying), mother (BLEEP)er
- See you never, (BLEEP)er
- Hasta la (BLEEP)ing vista, baby

I deeply apologize, this list has been fucking ruined by all the bleeps.

Fun Exercise #8 - Get Angry!

Write down your own personal ideas of how to literally say goodbye to the trash that hurt you! Remember, it's just junk; it has no feelings. Spit out all that anger or sadness in your heart and let your lips fly! Scream, get mad, cry, take out all your frustrations on it. Believe me, the junk deserves it, but you deserve to feel whole, loved, and clean. Declutter your heart! Also, if you're somehow a human being that's never been hurt once in your life, then cool! You can still come up with some fun insults to hurl at the junk as you throw it away.

EXERCISE# 8
GET ANGRY!

Date: ---------

Write down creative insults for your stuff, specially the ones that give you negative feelings!

"When you're following your inner voice, doors tend to eventually open for you, even if they mostly slam at first".

Kelly Cutrone

This is not limited to just objects that act as a source of pain for you. The things you get rid of should also be things you cherish; momentos of the past that hold only good memories. If you're married and your wedding dress has sat in your closet for a few years, ask yourself: do I ever plan to wear it again? If the answer is no, then sell it to save the money for your next anniversary or vacation. If the answer is yes, then put it away in a proper storage area in your home where it will be out of the way. This is applicable to all mementos that hold sentimental significance. Even when an object is gone, you will always still have the memory. You must put yourself before any of the materials in your home.

Fun Exercise #9 - Goodbye, Nostalgia!

Make a list of items below that hold sentimental value to you and plan to get rid of them. Take photos of the objects you're going to part with so that you do have some proof of them in your life, and ready yourself mentally to say goodbye. This is all for the best; make room in your life not just for your future but for your present as well.

EXERCISE# 9
GOODBYE. NOSTALGIA!

Date: ---------

My sentimental list:

"When defeat comes, accept it as a sign that your plans are not sound, rebuild Those plans, and set sail once more toward your coveted goal".

Napoleon Hill

Self Reflection 5

This part of getting rid of shit you don't need is, admittedly, pretty hard. Hell, getting rid of anything that you like a lot can feel that way. Take a short break to record your feelings here before you move on to taking back control of your house.

Fun Exercise #10 - Hasta la Vista!

Let's get to work! Over the next exercise, fill out what you're getting rid of and why, the last time you used the item you're throwing away, its most hated value, and whatever information you can remember about it.

EXERCISE# 10
HASTA LA VISTA!

Date: ------

I'm getting rid of	Because	Last time I used it

"Love is forgiving, accepting, moving on, embracing, and all encompassing. And if you're not doing that for yourself, you cannot do that with anyone else."

— Steve Maraboli

Think Ahead

Think back a couple of steps. Why did you pick this book up in the first place? Was it an unsubtle gift from a friend or family member? Did you buy it from a store? Did it magically manifest beneath a pile of clutter as if the mice living in your trash put it there as a means of intervention? If it's the last one, then yikes. If it's the other two, however, either you or the people you care about really think you have a problem. Because of this, it's important to start visualizing what your home will look like once it's finally in tip-top shape! Imagine your living room, kitchen, bathrooms, basement, backyard, attic, bedroom, storage closet, secret room you keep your most secretive secrets in—all of it, clean (and no longer a secret)! How much easier will it be to move around and even breathe in just by not being surrounded by mountains of crap you don't need? Visualization is key in any aspect of your life you want to be successful in, the least of which is a clean home.

Fun Exercise #11 - Dream House

Let's put pencil to paper! Use the space below to draw the rooms in your house in their current state. Then right beside it, draw it again without all the mess! This visual exercise is key to reaching your end goal as you proceed along with this book.

EXERCISE# 11
DREAM HOUSE

Date: ---------

Bedroom

Before

After

Please refer to the complete exercise# 11 in your booklet for the rest of the rooms.

"Life always begins with one step outside of your comfort zone".

Shannon L. Alder

Self Reflection 6

Before pushing forward, write more details down about how you could live your life out without being bogged down by clutter. What decorations do you want to see? What's your end goal? Even things unrelated to to cleaning your house matter in this case, as once your life gets tidied up literally, everything else will fall into place, as well.

Visualizing the Lifestyle of Your Dreams

Now that you've begun the process of decluttering, there's a pivotal question that you must ask yourself. "Why do I want to live a clutter-free life?" Of course, as I mentioned before, living in a place that looks like a murder of crows came through it is bad for your mental health, but that doesn't explain why *you* want to take control of your life. So, ask yourself: Why? What benefits do you reap by becoming cleaner, and ridding yourself of objects that you no longer have use for? Once you think of at least five reasons why your life should be decluttered, then you can begin to visualize the next step of the process.

Fun Exercise #12 - Why Should I Care About Being Clean?

In the space below, come up with no less than five reasons you want to live in a decluttered home. Why are you embarking on this journey? What motivates you to want to own less items you no longer use? If you're not sure what to write down, try referring to the Introduction pages; by rereading them and seeing that familiar scenario, you may just find the motivation you need to find your five reasons! Why do you want to see your home become cozy, relaxing, and comfortable?

EXERCISE# 12
WHY SHOULDI CARE ABOUT BEING CLEAN?

Date: ---------

Reason no. 1

No. 2

No. 3

No. 4

No. 5

"Hope in the shadow of fear is the worlds most powerful motivator."

Neal Shusterman

Now that you have your five reasons why you want a cleaner home, here comes the fun part! With sufficient motivation to get your ass in gear, you can start to visualize the kind of home you want! With the money you gain by selling items you're getting rid of; you'll have the funds to throw into decorating your space as soon as it's gotten its much-needed face-lift. Exactly how do you want to decorate it? Open up your Pinterest board or cut out pieces of magazines that inspire you with their showcasing of living spaces. Are you thinking you want to be a minimalist? Do you wanna go for that cozy cottage vibe? Or are you thinking of sharp, shimmering new upgrades to make your home super tech-savvy? Are you someone who believes diamonds are a girl's best friend, so you're gonna deck out every space with all manner of bling? Once you get rid of the junk, you're gonna be left with a blank canvas, so think of how incredible it'll look by the time you're all done with it!

Fun Exercise #13 - Pimp Yo' Space!

Let's make your home look chicer than an overpriced boutique! Once all that crap is out of your life, how are you going to redecorate your space? Are you gonna make your house the comfiest brick on the block? Or are you gonna finally dedicate areas for your hobbies? Maybe open up that storage room to make it into a bad-bitch style office? Using the space below, brainstorm all the things you could do with your house once it's all done being cleaned up. How you'll decorate it, how you'll organize everything, paint yourself your picture of your ideal home without clutter!

EXERCISE# 13
PIMP YO' SPACE!

Date: ---------

Visualize the home you want

**"I said "Somebody should do something about that".
Then I realized I am somebody".**

Lily Tomlin

Self Reflection 7

Take a break to write down how the process is going for you. Nothing is too little to write about, decluttering your own head is just as important as everything else!

Counting Your Possessions

Now that you're ready, let's put this shit into motion! In other words, c'mon, get rid of 'em! Grab the next thing you see, ask yourself: "Do I need this?" If the answer is no, the next question should be, "Do I love this?" If the answer is no, then TOSS IT IN THE TRASH, THE RECYCLING, DONATE IT OR SELL IT! If you do not absolutely love an object, you're going to tell it essentially, "You're FIRED!" It has served its purpose for you at one point, but now it's time to cut down on your "staff" of items in your home. Take out all any pent-up anger or frustration you have regarding your situation onto these disposable trinkets. You'll be going through each item, sorting them respectively, and then using an extra, super special, hidden option separate from the "trash, recycle, donate, sell" options. That hidden option. DESTRUCTION!

In recent years (recent as of the publication of this workbook) Destruction Therapy is a very well-practiced, and now celebrated means of literally taking out your feelings through violence! This is of course done in a safe environment, supervised by professionals. For the items you especially want to take your anger out on, I can't recommend it enough. Nothing is more cathartic than wringing yourself free of stress with a violent good time in one of these spaces. Good examples of places that exist where you can safely do this (provided you don't live out in the woods with lots of property, if you live there, just make sure you wear protection before you destroy anything!) is Therapy! Rage Room Mechanicsburg, Pennsylvania where you can bring your own items to destroy if you want among other things; and Break Room Therapy in West Michigan where you can bring your own breakables as well. Try looking up if there are any Destruction Therapy Rooms in your area.

Fun Exercise #14 - DESTROY!!

Try finding a Destruction Therapy Room near you. If you plan to go to one, great! Use the space below to plan out what items you're taking with you, how they matter to you, and why you want to destroy them! If you're not going to a destruction therapy room though, do you still want to destroy anything? If so, what do you plan to destroy? How? OR! If you don't want to destroy anything, explain why!

EXERCISE# 14
DESTROY!!

Date: ----------

Destruction therapy plan

"Do the hard jobs first. The easy jobs will take care of themselves."

Dale Carnegie

If violence isn't quite right for you in terms of physical aggression, then don't worry! There's still plenty else you can do to satisfy your frustrations. Now that you know of the destruction option, let's take a closer look at trashing, recycling, donating, or selling. Trashing and recycling speak for themselves, while selling is a slower process, and donations should only be for items that are usable or in acceptable condition. We've talked about these options already so instead of telling you how to do this, instead, we'll talk about HOW you address them as you get rid of them. Any clutter you part with, scream at it. Yes, you heard me. Shake it, scream at it, and insult it like it personally kicked you in the ass. You'll feel incredible once all that pent-up frustration is out and laid out, I know I absolutely did. "Fire" all the items you no longer have a need for. If you don't need it, don't love it, or MAYBE could see yourself needing it in six months: FIRE IT!

Fun Exercise #15 - Keeping Track

You don't need to catalogue every little thing you throw away like if it's an old candy wrapper but try to keep track of the items you throw away! The longer the list is, the more you'll see just how much space you're making for the rest of your life to happen. The more on this list, the better you'll feel to be happy you're rid of it in your life. Mark down if you're selling it, recycling it, or throwing it away.

EXERCISE# 15
KEEPING TRACK!

Date: ----------

I'm getting rid of	It will go to ☑			
	Recycle	Trash	Donate	Sell

"It has been my philosophy of life that difficulties vanish when faced boldly".

Isaac Asimov

Self Reflection 8

How did it feel to destroy that stuff? Wasn't it totally awesome?! Or did you choose not to destroy things? If so, why was that your specific choice? Tell me here about how and why you destroyed certain items instead of others, everything's safe her in this book!

The Genre Method

When it comes to finding a home for each individual item in your home, do you find that every room has a theme? The theme, of course, being kitchen, bedroom, etcetera? Unless you live in a studio apartment (in which case you could always designate by area) you probably do. However, are all the items exactly where they should be? Chances are that you have items of all categories strewn all-around your home. Magazines and books are meant to go on their respective shelves, but you may have some in the bathroom, on the coffee table, in your bedroom on the nightstand, or even in the kitchen (if it's a cookbook). Plates and dishes need to be put away in the cabinet, but all too often find themselves once again on the nightstand, the coffee table, or most egregiously the sink. The same can go for every object you can think of: lotions in the living room, medicine in the kitchen, pet toys under furniture—the point is, you more than likely have items scattered all over your house. So, rather than going through and donating/trashing/recycling/selling things room by room, instead, do it by *genre*.

For example, let's consider how we'll sort our books! You would gather up all the books and magazines in your house, then place them before you in a designated sorting area. Then, you go through each title and decide what you'll put in each respective pile to get rid of them or to place them back on the bookshelf. The best order for decluttering your home goes by wardrobe, paperwork, books/magazines, general items, then souvenirs. Quickly make your decision with each item but don't worry about putting anything away just yet, we'll get more into the idea of *organizing* by genre in chapter three. For now, focus on getting that crap out of your house!

Fun Exercise #16 - Genre Library

What genres are in your house? Write down each individual room you have (or designated area) and list some special things that should go to each genre.

EXERCISE# 16
GENRE LIBRARY

Date: ---------

I found it in	Main Genres: note down things you found in each room that should go to:				
	Wardrobe	paperwork	Books	souvenirs	Others
Living room					
Kitchen					
Bedroom					
Washrooms					

"It's not always that we need to do more but rather that we need to focus on less".

Nathan W. Morris

Becoming a Role Model

Once you start to declutter your belongings, you'll find that others will notice a difference in you. "What's your secret?" your co-worker asks, "Do you have a partner now? Did you get your haircut? Did you lose weight?!" While all of these may (or may not) be true, the truth is the difference they're seeing comes from your very own hard work. Not just co-workers either, but friends and family, those that genuinely care about you will see how much more energy you have. When they ask you if something about you has changed, you can tell them, "No, but I changed myself."

This is where you can really become a pioneer for your loved ones by telling them exactly what you've been up to. Let them know how you threw away that harmonica your first-ever partner gave to you, or how thanks to digging through old boxes of junk that you've found the CUTEST trinket ever that you sold for hundreds of dollars. Let them know that you've made a decision to make your life better by getting rid of as much as you can, as quickly as you can. Pretty soon, they're going to start thinking they should do the same thing, too! Even better, they're gonna look to you for advice as to what to get rid of and how. Set up constant communication with your friends or family members when they commit to this same lifestyle so that you and they can talk about all the new trends in upcycling your garbage! Nothing is more satisfying than giving advice to someone who once doubted your ability to let things go, so prove those people wrong by feeding them ten slices of humble pie. Speaking of upcycling, don't worry if you can't sell things or can't give them away so easily! If it can't fit in the trash, try passing it off to a family member, friend, or co-worker instead.

The Best Time to Declutter Is in the Morning!

Shoutout to all my early birds! The most productive time slot of the day is early morning, use this to your advantage when you first wake up to get right to work! Try setting out your garbage bags, lists, anything you need to get started on your day the night before rather than scrambling in the dark to find your gear. It is hard to wake up sometimes first thing in the morning, so try to change your alarm tone to be something poppy, as waking up with a good mindset is crucial to your journey! For those of you who are night owls, tough luck! Just kidding, try to wake up at sunrise so you have the waning rays of daylight to act as your fuel before setting to work. At this time when you're getting started, put on classical music or at least melodies without lyrics. Only use pieces of media that won't distract you from the task at hand and will keep you in the mood to be productive! For those who are deaf or hard of hearing, plan to have a film playing in the background with subtitles that you don't need to pay attention to.

Fun Exercise #17 - Ready the Equipment!

Alright, let's lay out our gear! In the exercise below, we're going to list out our tools! This checklist for you will involve the following: What sorting supplies you need, what clothes you'll wear, your meal plan for your day of decluttering, the playlist or film you've picked out to keep on while you tidy, and so on. Then make sure it's all laid out for you so the moment you wake up, you're ready to kick ass.

EXERCISE# 17
READY THE EQUIPMENT!

Date: ---------

Tools

- Supplies (i.e cleaning tools, recycle, trash, sell and donate bins, sticky notes etc.).

- Clothes (i.e. what I'm gonna wear during decluttering activities).

- Meal Plan (i.e. simple and easy meals for the decluttering day).

- Playlist (i.e. what I'm gonna listen to. TIP: try something with no lyrics like classic music, and avoid catchy songs to stay focused).

Please refer to the exercise# 17 in your booklet to check off the list.

**"It's not that some people have willpower, and some don't…
It's that some people are ready to change and others are not".**

James Gordon

Self Reflection 9

Are you a morning person, or a night person? Are you someone who feels more productive earlier rather than later? If you're a night owl, do you wish to be a morning dove or vice versa? How will you use time to effectively work in your favour based on your biological clock?

CHAPTER THREE: ORGANIZING BY GENRE

Are you ready to have your mind completely blown away? Be given some life-altering information that will eventually save you hours upon hours of time? Well, look no further, because you've come to the right place! Thanks to the egregious amount of time I've spent mastering this craft, I've discovered the one thing that has always saved my ass: organizing by genre. But wait, I hear you say, you already talked about that! Well shut up for a second and I'll tell you more about how you'll use it not to throw shit away, but to keep the things you actually still have!

Now, at this point, you should have thrown away all the crap you don't need or have a use for. If you haven't thrown anything away: shame on you! By this point, your clutter should already have seen a massive decrease thanks to your work in chapter two. If you didn't, get back in line! Seriously, this step can only be done without any of the crap you had before. Get your ass in gear and move it for the sake of your own sanity! I'll wait right here until you're done.

...While I wait though, **here's a tip:** if due to your clutter you have some bugs, or specifically flies hanging around, get that shit outta here. To do this, just fill a shallow cup or basin with a small amount of apple cider vinegar, then add a drop of dish soap to the top (don't mix them together). Leave it sitting out where your fly problem is at its worst and watch the flies come buzzing. The sweet smell of the apple cider vinegar to them is the equivalent of a fresh piece of fruit with the flesh exposed, they'll come right for it. The drop of dish soap will break the tension of the vinegar, so those assholes will drop right in and drown. Voila! You have your own, sustainably made fly trap. No bullshit chemicals, no bad smells for you (unless you hate vinegar), and clean-up is as easy as dumping the evidence down the drain.

Are you done going through chapter two by now? Finally, I was waiting here forever, it was starting to get really awkward. Anyway, if you're ready to have your mind freaking blown, here's the rub: organizing by genre is gonna save your ass when it comes to taking less time to get your stuff together. Seriously, this is a time-travel style method that will give you the opportunity to explore your past, present, and future by assessing all your collected possessions over the years. Once you've made your analysis and said, "Ah, yes, this is all my shame laid out before me," then you're gonna decide what will go and what will stay. Your decision on either end should be determined by the lifestyle we visualized back in chapter two. Does your kitschy, nonsensical kitchen gadget you got from your mom last Christmas REALLY fit into the French country vibe you want for your kitchen, or are you just holding onto it because mom gave it to you? Did that purchase from Amazon for Christmas lights pay off when instead of decorating with them, you shoved them into the back of a drawer? Did your newly found hobby in making robots out of Legos ever pick up or is that box full of booby traps sitting forgotten in a corner? In short: keep only what will help you paint the picture of your ideal lifestyle in your home. The rest, as they say, is just tchotchke.*

*Before you google that word: tchotchke (pronounced Chah-ch-key) is an inexpensive souvenir, trinket, or ornament.

Fun Exercise #18 - Tchotchke

What tchotchke do you have in your home? Where did you get it from? In this exercise, you're going to analyse any trinkets or bobbles you have and where you got them from. Then get rid of them! You don't need no freakin' tchotchke!

EXERCISE# 18
TCHOTCHKE

Date: ---------

Tchotchke list (and where did you get it from):

"You can fool everyone else, but you can't fool your own mind".

David Allen

Step One: Your Wardrobe!

First things first, let's catalogue all the clothes you own! That's right, we're gonna inventory every scrap of clothing you own. Below, add to each individual list a short description of the clothes you have. Don't worry if you run out of room, there'll be extra space to fill in at the end of this list if you need to! Get your ass in gear and dump all those clothes where you can sort them! Remember: right now you are JUST cataloguing these items. By taking heck load inventory you can see just how much you might have stuffed away that you didn't even think about. As you go along, also remember to write down how you feel about the piece. Is it old? New? Never been worn? Make sure you write down the condition of the piece in addition to whether or not you like it as well as when you last wore it, if ever.

Here's an example of what it might look like:

Dress - Midi A-line with purple sequins - New with tags - Never worn - Love it!

T-shirt - Pink Floyd graphic - Old, has holes - Worn yesterday - Love it!

Sweater - Plain red - Fairly used - Worn last year - Don't like it

Fun Exercise #19 - Clothing Inventory

EXERCISE# 19
CLOTHING INVENTORY

Date: ---------

Please refer to the exercise# 19 in your booklet for additional space for all clothing types:

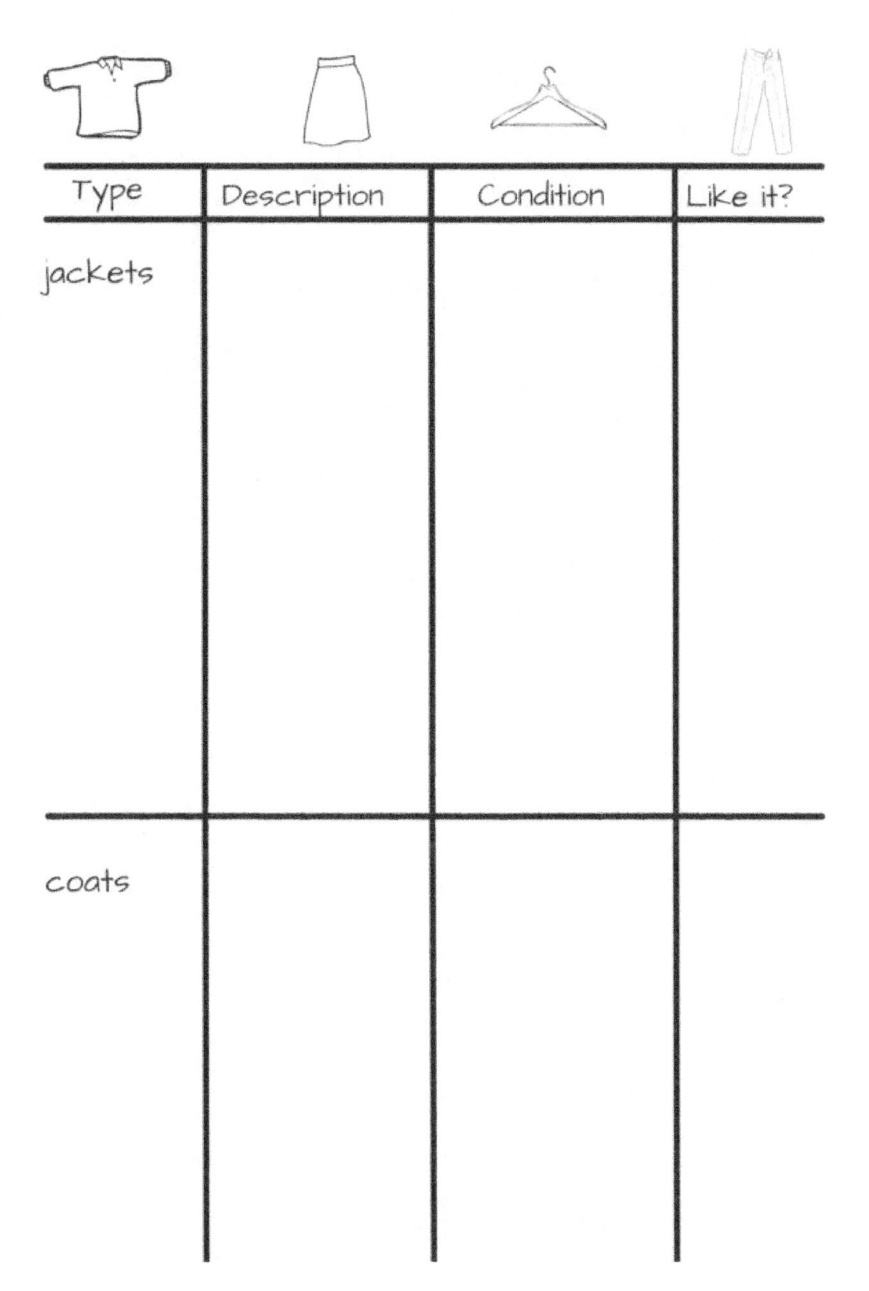

Type	Description	Condition	Like it?
jackets			
coats			

"Simplicity boils down to two steps:
Identify the essential.
Eliminate the rest".

Leo Babauta

Self Reflection 10

This is where the going gets tough, and the tough get going. How are going to continue to motivate yourself to do what you know needs to be taken care of? Don't sit on your ass and expect the problems to go away, from now on the work is all about you, you , you! So, keep on running-or just write about running instead. That's what I usually do!

By the time you're finished compiling all your items into a few piles, you'll be shocked by the volume and amount of clothing that you own! That's a lot, right? Well, don't worry! I've got a great way to help you figure out what to keep and what not to, it's gonna be a heck load of fun! First, take a good long look at your list. Huge, right? Well, what's nice about how you catalogued everything is you know a little bit about every tiny detail! In order to cut back on the amount of crap in your wardrobe, you have to know what you're gonna keep versus what you're not going to.

First things first, anything on that list that was something you didn't love, cross it out! If there was something on that list with holes, cross that out too! Then take those clothes out of your original pile and chuck them into their respective bin among the recycle/trash/donate/sell piles! Now you're left with only clothes that you love that are in good condition. That means throwing away your favourite ugly band t-shirt with more holes in it than was originally intended, sorry-not-sorry. No one wants to see your ass looking like it got attacked by moths and mice at the supermarket, there's already plenty of people there suffering from that exact condition. You're cuter than that, so act like it, dammit! Remember to hold onto any seasonal clothing that you love, you'll need it later after all. Dat ass only stays fine in tight miniskirts around summer and turns into a butt-sicle come winter.

Now that you're left with only the clothing you love, remake that same list with your new catalogue of gorgeous clothing that expresses who you truly are. There will be less space this time because you don't need to keep track of the items you don't love!

Fun Exercise #20 - (Diet) Clothing Inventory

Alright, way to kick ass and take names! You've come so far already, but we're not quite done. This is the fun part: using your list and your shortened pile of clothing, assemble in your mind how you'll wear them. That's right! For each season with your remaining clothing, you're going to design five outfits apiece using what you have in your wardrobe. This will inspire you to continue wearing only quality threads that you love and never settle for less. There's nothing wrong with going out in sweater and sweatpants, sure, but let's commit to kicking this shit up a notch! This is YOUR makeover, so you're gonna treat yourself like the piece of fine royalty you are. Once your house is completely clean, you're gonna rock your new style. So, shed that outer lining of your chrysalis and become that fine butterfly-lookin' bitch you know you are!

EXERCISE# 20
(DIET) CLOTHING INVENTORY

Date: ----------

Please refer alos to exercise# 20 in your booklet, as you'll find additional space for all clothing types:

Type	Description	Condition	Like it?
jackets			
coats			
Blouses			

"A challenge only becomes an obstacle when you bow to it".

Ray A. Davis

Fun Exercise #21 - C'mon, Vogue!

Now that you feel inspired, it's time to put those amazing outfits away! You can feel free to tear out those pages and put them somewhere where you won't forget those adorable outfits you made. Use them as inspiration for the next time you head out depending on what season you're in! I personally prefer the folding method over putting things in the closet. The only thing I recommend hanging up in the closet are dresses, suits, and coats. Putting things onto a hanger and into the closet, especially if it's your entire wardrobe, can take up a lot of space you can use for other things. A cluttered space is a cluttered mind, so what does it mean when your closets are the things in your house that are stuffed full? It means you gotta get rid of the overstuffing and let your clothes breathe a little! Choose the drawers you want to put away everything in, throw away any straggler socks that have no mate. By the end of this step, your closet will look brand-spanking new.

EXERCISE# 21
C`MON, VOGUE!

Date: ----------

Please refer to exercise# 21 in your booklet for worksheets for other year seasons:

This is what I'm gonna wear:

Winter Outfits

Outfit #1

Outfit #2

Outfit #3

Outfit #4

Outfit #5

"Sometimes, things may not go your way, but the effort should be there every single night."

Michael Jordan

Self Reflection 11

In the spaces below, take a moment to pencil down your thoughts. How does it feel to have your wardrobe completely cleaned out? Are you excited about the outfits you've found in your own closet? Spill at your closet-stuffed secrets here to get them off your chest!

A SHORT MESSAGE FROM THE AUTHOR

Hey, are you enjoying the book? I'd love to hear your thoughts!

Many readers do not know how hard reviews are to come by, and how much they help an author.

I would be incredibly grateful if you could take just 60 seconds to write a brief review on Amazon, even if it's just a few sentences!

>> Leave a review on Amazon US <<

>> Leave a review on Amazon UK <<

Step Two: Books and Magazines!

By now, you should be familiar with the process of figuring out what you love, what you hate, and what you just tend to keep around for the sake of keeping around. With your familiarity to this process thanks to step one, this part will be a piece of cake! Unlike sorting the wardrobe though, there are some smaller factors to consider when handling books or magazines and where they should go. First of all, try to put absolutely nothing in the trash if you can help it. If you have old books, only put those in the donate pile. See if your local library wants them, otherwise, take them to the thrift store. The resell value on books is shit unless it's a textbook, in that case, try to sell them! Old magazines, if they have no value due to being a collector's item, should be recycled. Do your part for mother earth before we all die in a fiery blaze or something.

There's a Japanese word, a term which means "purchasing a stack or collection of books that you have not read." This word is "tsundoku" and is pronounced tsoon-dough-ku with the "ts" being like the first part of the word "tsunami." Which is quite accurate now that I think about it. For those of us who are book collectors out there, have you ever looked at your assortment of books and thought, "man, if this ever fell on me, it'd be like a tidal wave of knowledge and I'd drown under it like I was sucked into a tsunami?" No, just me? Okay then. Well, now imagine it so I don't have to be embarrassed outing myself to be a nerd that likes to read. Imagine, if you do have a book collection, being trapped when all your books fall on you. How many of those books have you actually read? How many of those books were just filling up space on your shelf? How many times have you said, "Oh, yeah, I'll totally get around to reading it," and then rewatched "The Office" for the third time instead?

Now, I know I'm calling you out here. It can be difficult to part with books most of all but consider this. If you have books that you really want to read and will as soon as the house is being done and cleaned, you can keep those! But for those titles, you bought with stagnated interest that you *might* read them one day, screw 'em! Bring them to your local library as donations. Then, if you ever get wild, you can always go back to the library and check them out to read them! Provided you're not a jerk that never returns their library books, that is. If you don't, get those freakin' books back to your library!!!

Fun Exercise #22 - Sexy Librarian Role Play

Now that you're ready, grab some empty boxes and get ready! You're gonna sort through and catalogue every book you have. Mark down if you've read them, if you haven't, if you've ever wanted to, and where you got them from. Unlike clothes, there's not too much romanticism this time. Just mark down whether you'll recycle, donate, or sell them! Then, once you're done cataloguing, sort them away using your new, handy list! Don't worry about any loose paperwork you might have, that will become relevant in the next step.

EXERCISE# 22
SEXY LIBRIARIAN ROLE PLAY

Date:--------

Book name	It will go to ☑			
	Recycle	Trash	Donate	Sell

"The tragedy in life doesn't lie in not reaching your goal.
The tragedy lies in having no goal to reach".

Benjamin E. Mays

Step Three: The Fine Print!

Now, here comes probably the messiest aspect of this whole organizing schtick. For every loose paper on the ground, in piles, on your desk, old mail shoved into drawers, or useless information put into a filing cabinet, you're probably looking at a few hours' time of sorting. Announcements, letters, manuals, flyers, expired coupons, advertisements, newspapers, bank statements, and payslips are all littered around your house like the world's most boring paper trail. These pieces of paper are also likely bits of your information, your signature, and a whole lot of crap that would be primed for any burglar breaking in to steal your identity or bank accounts. For that reason, almost every single bit of it has to go!! First things first: rounding all of the loose-leafs up.

Fun Exercise #23 - Unsexy Janitor Role Play

Finding every single piece of paper, you have in your house is super involved, so try to get everything at once! Make a sweep of your home, checking every single room and nook or cranny you may have shoved papers in. I'm talking drawers, shelves, closets, piles, under sofa cushions, under the sofa itself, and ESPECIALLY under the bed. Leave no stone unturned as you move about the house collecting every single scrap you see! Bring a trash bag with you to pick up and discard any torn pieces of paper, candy wrappers, or other shit you have laying around as you go. Below, make a list of all the rooms of your house and check them off when you've thoroughly searched each one for paperwork. Be sure to designate a single area, likely in the living room, where you can set down the piles of papers as you find them. Also, if you have some important papers already filed away somewhere, bring them out as well from whatever place you've stored them in. You'll need them for the sorting process.

EXERCISE# 23
UNSEXY JANITOR ROLE PLAY

Date: ---------

Make sure you check off each room after you clear it from all paperwork ✓

- ☐ Living Room
- ☐ Bedroom
- ☐ Hallways
- ☐ Kids Room
- ☐ Basement
- ☐ Kitchen
- ☐ Additional Room
- ☐ Additional Room

"If you spend too much time thinking about a thing, you'll never get it done."

Bruce Lee

Self Reflection 12

I marked down that earlier exercise as being a sexy librarian role-play because screw it, why not dress up and look cute while you do your work? Maybe by pretending you have someone to impress with your looks you'll feel motivated to stick out your butt further than usual and do some squats to work those fancy glutes of yours! The exercise after that called the unsexy janitor role-play is really just how I feel when picking up after others when they decide they don't want to do it themselves. Hostage, relatable…?

Great, now that you have all the paperwork together, try to begin sorting things out and placing them in respective piles: Trash, recycle, and keep. The only things you should be keeping are important documents like the deed to your house, the title of your car, birth certificate, social security stuff, taxes—you get the idea. Almost everything else should go into the trash or recycling bin depending on whatever the material is made of. I'm always an advocate for putting what I can into recycling so they can be reused, but that should only happen if the paper isn't blemished by something like food or drink stains, much less anything else that's unsavoury. For any paperwork that isn't literally life-altering, ask yourself: Do you need it now? Should you keep them *forever?* I am not at all a fan of filing systems unless they're in an office space, but it is important to keep it organized. Once you've sorted through everything between what's important versus what to throw away, pick ONE, I repeat, ONE (1) location to store the important documents in. Ensure this location is secure, in a spot you won't forget about them, and one you can access freely. That way, the next time you need to grab these important papers you'll know *exactly* where to find them. The last thing you need is to be digging through fifteen drawers to find out exactly what you put down for last year's taxes.

Step Four: Everything Else!

What, did you expect me to hold your hand the entire way? This is the ULTIMATE NO-NONSENSE GUIDE, not the ULTIMATE GENTLY TELL YOU YOU'RE A SPECIAL SNOWFLAKE GUIDE. Listen up, from here on, you're gonna make your own genre and organize from there. Aside from the previous three categories we just did, it's time for you to step up and take charge. Think about the genres you need to organize things that belong in the kitchen, bathroom, living room. Do you need to sort your old bedsheets and general linens, pick through the towels to see what's old and ratty versus what can stay? Is your hobby room in desperate need of picking apart the endless pile of yarn, hidden crochet-slash-knitting needles, spools of thread? Maybe your hobby is collectibles; action figures, pennies, dolls, buttons—you get the idea. Everyone has their own genres from the broadest room categories to the tiniest of trinkets.

Fun Exercise #24 - The Great Shit-Get-Ridder

So, what you're going to do is over the next dozen pages, you're gonna make genres that span your ENTIRE household, and for each genre, you're going to catalogue everything you find, then sort through it for what to put in the trash, recycle, sell, or donate.

Here's a list of possible genres you can use:
- Kitchen supplies
- Electrical equipment
- Medicine
- Tools
- Hobby items
- Pantry
- Drawer contents
- Pet toys and supplies
- Candles and fragrance-makers such as incense
- Bathroom supplies
- Music collections (Vinyl's, CD's, instruments...)
- Exercise equipment
- Anything else you can think of!

The world's your oyster for this one. After you're done sorting everything that you can come up with, we still have one more step that I urge you to not yet do anything with until you're done with this:

the category of nostalgia. For now, do everything you can. Move your ass, and get it done!

EXERCISE# 24
THE GREAT SHIT-GET-RIDDER

Date: ---------

Genre/items	It will go to ☑			
	Recycle	Trash	Donate	Sell

"The only thing standing between you and your goal is the bullshit story you keep telling yourself as to why you can't achieve it".

Jordan Belfort

Self Reflection 13

Take a short break to record your thoughts on all this cataloguing and disposing of items. How are you feeling? How does it feel to see your life decluttered? Do you feel empowered, or a little lost in the mess? If so, don't worry about it, soon your place will have more room in it than you'll know what to do with.

Fun Exercise #24 - The Great Shit-Get-Ridder Continued...

Remember that as time goes on, you may not have the same use for things you once did. It might be easy at first to hesitate, to want to hold onto the things that you worked hard to earn. However, after a time, things simply have no use in your home other than taking up space. You may just be surprised by how little you have left by the end of this. Feel liberated by the things that no longer weigh you down. The more you throw away, the lighter the weight of the world becomes. The things you once purchased that brought you joy have long served their purpose, and thus no longer have any use. The same goes for gifts, as well. That topic does, however, bring us to the final step of this chapter.

Step Five: The Nostalgic Plug!

This final step in this chapter may just be the hardest. While cleaning, you may have come across old items that used to hold a lot of sentimental value for you—set them aside rather than get rid of them. Old letters, drawings from kindergarten, toys, greeting cards, and so on. Perhaps a gift from an old lover, or a parent that's no longer with you. At one time, the purpose they served was to warm your heart. Now, the only purpose they serve is to take up precious space in your home. So, you know what time it is: That's right it's time to get rid of it.

Pack that sad shit into a garbage sack and toss it into the closest dumpster. Maybe set the dumpster on fire, too. Okay, don't do that. But do push the dumpster down an empty hill. Okay, fine, don't do that either. It's against the "law," or whatever. Anyway, memories are nice and all, but you already have those in your head. The fact is nostalgia can add piles upon piles to an already impossible amount of clutter. So, just do yourself a favour and don't have it around. Easier said than done, sure. I think I mentioned it way earlier, but you can always take photos of the things you hold dear before you get rid of them. That way you'll always have those precious memories, but those items will be out of your home, and thus out of your life.

Nostalgia, when it comes to clutter, is nothing but the clog in the drain of the cesspool of the mess. When you clear it out, you'll have beautiful, clear, flowing water (metaphorically speaking) that flushes away all the negativity right where it belongs, down the freaking drain. Unclog your life and commit to getting rid of the past before it completely undermines all your attempts to move forward into the future.

Fun Exercise #25 - Unclog Your Future

Alrighty, don't make me repeat myself. Get your ass in gear and get to work, you know the drill! Catalog everything, only this time write down if you'll take a photo of it before you throw it away with selling, donating, recycling, or actually trashing it!

EXERCISE# 25
UNCLOG YOUR FUTURE

Date:........

Sentimental item	It will go to ☑				
	Recycle	Trash	Donate	Sell	Photo taken?

117

"Until we can mange time, we can manage nothing else".

Peter Drucker

Now that you've gone through the process of getting this shit out of your life, you'll really have had time to discover yourself through your possessions. By deciding what to keep versus what to get rid of, you'll have discovered how you really base your decisions. Do you choose to keep things based on a certain look? A theme that resonates with what you've visualized before? What new goals are you hoping to achieve with the remainder of the items you possess? With what you have now, how will the things you own help you get to what you want?

By relieving your life of all the clutter, the burdens of owning them will completely wash away. Your life will get easier. Your mind and soul will make better decisions. Heck, you might even notice the metamorphosis already! With less crap to trip over, your stress levels will go down astronomically. That means shit like acne, back pain, headaches, and a couple of other symptoms might be going away or improving. Stress is a killer and living in a cluttered home only adds to the myriad of troubles to pile it on. Now that your home has that much less crap to worry about, the only question is where do you go from here?

Fun Exercise #26 - Fuzzy Feelings and Other Crap

Last time cataloguing for this chapter, promise. Trust me, this shit is getting old for me too! Basically, now you're just gonna go through every item you own. Don't trash or get rid of anything, you're just gonna talk about how these items make you feel. For example, do you love your coffee table? How do you feel about your dining set? This is to get you thinking about how you'd like to keep, or eventually replace, the items you still have.

EXERCISE# 26
FUZZY FEELINGS AND OTHER CRAP

Date:--------

Item	It will go to ✓					Condition	Like it?
	Recycle	Trash	Donate	Sell		

121

"Motivation is the fuel necessary to keep the human engine running".

Zig Ziglar

Self Reflection 14

Damn this chapter was a slog to get through, right?! Wrong! I bet you had an absolute blast getting rid of all the shit you don't need anymore! If you didn't, then you need to take control by making this process more fun for yourself. Buck up, suck it up, cheer up, and shut up because we're not quite done yet! By ripping off the proverbial band-aid and getting things done, you've already taken a whole lot of steps to improve your life as you know it. Still, it can be pretty exhausting, even if it was a fun time. So, let's take a short break while you jot down your thoughts, sing my praises, or just grumble. The only person who'll read it is you. After all!

CHAPTER FOUR: NOW LET'S ORGANIZE WHAT IS LEFT, OR "WHAT YOU REALLY LOVE!"

Congratu-freaking-lations, you're done!!! Well, with the decluttering part of it, anyway. If you're not, then what the hell are you doing here? Go away! Go start over and think about what you've done! Alright, now that you've ACTUALLY got a house that doesn't look like a rat king's nest atop a garbage dump, celebrate a little! Do a little dance, eat some shitty fast food, I don't care, whatever. Just don't go buying anything NEW yet, capiche?! That's part of the freaking problem, not the solution! Anyway, the point is that the hardest part of this is all done. Good for you, all it took was a damn book to tell you to get your shit together. Yay! Jokes aside, I'm proud of you for making it this far. You're really impressive, not many people can do what you have! That's why so many people's houses look like garbage!! Not yours though, good for you!

Now is a good time to take a moment. Take a breath, look around you. Your house is so much clearer than it was before, and it's all thanks to your hard work. Well, there is just one problem though. Uh, and that is, YOUR HOUSE STILL LOOKS LIKE SHIT!!! "But how is this possible?!" You may ask. Well, here's the kicker: You just got RID of all the shit you didn't need, and that's awesome! But now you're stuck with what's left. Oof, maybe cry about it a little. If you're done feeling miffed though, it's time to face the facts: You're not done yet. Yeah, yeah, I know, that sucks since you just worked really hard, but hey, you're almost done! That's something to be proud of. Don't worry, at this point, I was also feeling like tearing my freakin' hair out too. Here's the bad news: You still need to organize and clean up your home even if it has less stuff in it. Here's the good news, though! Because you have less stuff, doing this part is gonna go by in a snap!

Fun Exercise #27 - Oops, You're Not Done!

Namaste, bitches! We're gonna figure out how to align your centre by finding a *centre* for each individual item after this! For now, though, survey your home. How does it look with less stuff? How can it be improved? DO NOT CLEAN YET. Just look and figure out what you need to do with your stuff! All you're doing now is brainstorming, getting the gears in your head turning about how you could tidy up.

EXERCISE# 27
OOPS, YOU`RE NOT DONE!

Date: ---------

Cleaning Time

Walk into each room and start to put a quick plan for each one of how it will look like in its final shape and how you will clean it:

- For Living room, my plan is:

- For Bedroom, my plan is:

- For Kitchen, my plan is:

- For Kids room, my plan is:

- For Basement, my plan is:

Before we really get into the meat of this chapter, let me lay some things down for you. First of all, now that you have less stuff, you may have noticed a few… unsavoury things. Things like spilled soda that the ants have rejoiced in by slurping their tiny mandibles against as they march in through that crack in the wall, which is hella gross. Or maybe you've found an unfortunate pile your pet has left as an accident, also gross! Perhaps the worst though… the dreaded, "what colour is this supposed to be?" If you're thinking that when you're looking at your shower, your tub, your sink, the toilet, an article of clothing, your carpet, a stuffed animal, or so on… THAT'S NASTY!! THAT IS SUPER NASTY!

So, what do you do? Man, you really gotta look into this book for all the answers, huh? It's simple: *bring the weapons.* Before you go reaching for your guns in the safe or your katana collection (you nerd), I'm not talking about arms of the battlefield variety. Although trying to watch someone clean a toilet with a war hammer would make for an excellent viral video, you're here to get *rid* of anything that could be viral. After the great fuckening of 2020, you'd be out of your mind to *not* want to scrub everything clean until it sparkled, and then spray it with another layer of disinfectant for good measure. Even if you don't believe in the great fuckening of 2020 for whatever reason, there's no denying one simple fact: We as human beings are DISGUSTING. For all the farting, eating, vomiting, belching, using the toilet—whatever that we do that's inherent to human nature—there's a mess left in our wake. That's just life, and that's what it means to be alive. That's right, you heard it here: living is gross.

However, you could very easily make it, you know, less gross. To do this, as we go about organizing everything remaining in our house, you're gonna need to bring with you your arsenal of cleaning tools. This doesn't have to be anything fancy, and it doesn't have to cost you any money. First of all, if you don't have any cleaning supplies, get some. You can find appropriate cleaners at the dollar store, along with sponges, laundry detergents, whatever the hell you need. That being said, if you're in a pinch, here's a lifesaver tip for you: you can make a multipurpose cleaner that cleans literally anything with just dish soap and water. Do I recommend it for scrubbing your greasy fingerprints off of mirrors? No, definitely not, but for most surfaces, you really can't go wrong with the combination. I'd still say invest in dollar store cleaners for cheap cleaning fluids. Or, if you're like me and wanna save the planet, go for a more sustainable option by doing research and picking up all-natural cleaning chemicals for slightly more money. Look, the point is, you're gonna need some shit to get started.

Also, one more thing before we go to our next fun exercise. Sometimes, cheap does not mean sustainable. There are times where you'll pick up some sponges, or a mop, or a broom for a great price, only to find when you get home that the mop doesn't clean well, or the sponges turn to shreds the moment you use them to scrub your dishes. I encourage you to bypass the cheapest of the cheap if you can swing it, and invest in the good shit. Again, do your research, and don't start running to your car to buy the next $1,000 vacuum or anything, I'm just saying be smart about what you get and how you use it.

Fun Exercise #28 - Shove It Up Your Arsenal

Gather your equipment, what will you bring with you as you go about organizing? What brands do you have? Would you prefer to swap it out for something more natural? Whatever you have, list the chemicals and other cleaning equipment you can use at your disposal. Have them on hand with you when you go about organizing your house! If you don't have something on this checklist, make an effort to get them. This is basic adult shit you will need to maintain your brand new, made-over house.

EXERCISE# 28
SHOVE IT UP YOUR ARSENAL

Date: ---------

Check off what you have and add more as needed

- Broom
- Mop
- Sponges
- Toilet scrubber
- Plunger
- Soap
- Toilet paper

Self Reflection 15

Just by the way, exactly how is your house looking anyway? Have you noticed anything... icky as you got rid of your excess crap? Do you see any splatters on the walls? Spilled coffee you forgot about? An easter egg you didn't manage to locate until it was too late to get rid of the smell? If not, take a closer look at everything. Your walls, after all, are not meant to look like Picasso decided to work with spaghetti sauce instead of oil paints.

Great, now you've got everything you need—or are going to get what you need. I highly recommend you move your cute little ass and get the shit you need BEFORE this because what you're gonna do is scrub as you organize. That means, for example, when taking care of organizing the genre of things that go in drawers, you take EVERYTHING out of the drawer, then scrub it down, then organize everything back into the drawer. You're getting rid of all the debris, gross germs, and disgusting little spatters of shit you didn't think about before.

Right, now that that's settled, let's get started for real. What happens next is you're gonna pick out your genres again from before, only instead of trashing, donating, selling, or recycling your items, you're going to just organize them as they should be. Once this step is done, you're going to basically be set for the rest of your life—so long as you live here, anyway. When something has found its proper home in your household, there's no reason your clutter should ever get as severe as it had been. The end goal of this part of the workbook is that once you're finished, you'll never have to do it again (except maybe to a much smaller extent once or twice a year). You'll always be able to keep your home in order with just minimal effort, with maybe five minutes a day putting anything away from here on out. So, let's shake a tailfeather and get started!

Fun Exercise #29 - Fixing the Genre for Good!

To begin, try to recall those genres you made before, how you sorted the clutter to get rid of everything you could back in chapter three. You can use the same genres now. For example, put anything related to the TV such as game consoles, remotes, sound systems, cables, and so on with the entertainment system. Anything kitchen-related, wash it and put it away where it belongs like in kitchen cupboards or drawers. Below, list the genres you used before. Then, start cleaning them. Check them off your list as you go so that you keep track of your progress. Be sure to scrub down all the surfaces you can with your cleaning products, too! Don't worry too much about vacuuming or sweeping through the spaces that may need them. That will come later! For now, focus on washing the containers as you organize things.

EXERCISE# 29
FIXING THE GENRE FOR GOOD!

Date: ---------

Cleaning Checklist
Write down items you cleaned

- ☑ Cleaned
- ☐ -------------
- ☐ -------------
- ☐ -------------
- ☐ -------------
- ☐ -------------
- ☐ -------------
- ☐ -------------
- ☐ -------------

While you organize, bear in mind that wherever you store your remaining belongings, that's where they're going to stay as long as you have them. Keep the kitchen supplies in their proper area, so when you need a can opener you know exactly where it is. Even more, make sure that items you always need to grab before you leave the house such as your wallet, watch, keys, camera, shoes, bag, glasses, and so on are all in one spot. This way, when you leave your home, if something is near that area that you need to bring with you for whatever reason such as a gift for a friend, a receipt for a return, or some clipped coupons, you know that those are the items you need to bring with you before you go. That way, the next time you ask yourself "where are my keys?" You'll know exactly where they are—and if they're not there, shame on you, asshole, you haven't learned your lesson. Make it your ritual whenever you get home to take your keys out of your purse or pocket and put them in the area they ALWAYS need to be. Then put away your wallet or purse wherever that is meant to go too. For those that use purses, this has the added benefit of being able to easily swap out the contents of the purses if you like to rotate them often.

This goes just as well for almost any other item you can think of. Need the remote? It must be in the box by the television. Need the garage door opener? It must be in the laundry room, and so on.

Fun Exercise #30 - Giving Everything a Home

Now that everything is organized as it should be, is it WHERE it should be? Below, you're going to decide exactly where you're going to put every important object to you, and then you'll make that space. For example: Where do you plan to always put your house keys from now on? If that area doesn't exist yet, make one using the items you already have, such as a pretty bowl or bin by the door. Make sure EVERYTHING important to you has its own, designated spot. I'll write down some things for you that might be important, in case they don't come to mind! This list has an added bonus, if you forget where something is, you can always refer to this list to see where it SHOULD be. Over time, it'll become so easy to remember where everything is that it will become second nature—or even better, muscle memory.

EXERCISE# 30
GIVING EVERYTHING A HOME

Date:-------

Sorting & Organizing time

Item	I Will keep it at:
Keys	
Mail	
Wallet	
Purses	
Important Documents	
Remote controls	
China	
Perfumes	
Air fresheners	
Cleaning equipment	
Tools	

Self Reflection 16

At this point, your house should really start to look like it's coming together. You've been working your ass off, so now it's beginning to seem like there's a light at the end of this long-ass tunnel.

Congrats! You should take a load off for a bit before wrapping up. Treat yourself to a cold soda or a small sweet treat. How do you intend to treat yourself? Or would you prefer to just push on?

HOLD IT! Before we go any further, ask yourself: Have I cleaned the inside of my refrigerator in a while? Did I blow out my garage? What does the inside of my car look like? Now that those areas you started on are all organized and clean, you can't forget the areas that you may have missed! Storage areas count, like attics or basements. The inside of your car could be a total, gross hot mess full of spilled drinks and crap on the floorboard, or worse, a bunch of clutter you haven't gotten rid of! Without moving forward, you need to make sure you scrub out every nook and cranny you have. After all, a clean home means EVERYTHING you have is clean! Take some time to scrub out your car, wash the exterior, clean out your air conditioning, and sort out your fridge! This stuff can be easy to forget about, but it's also a part of everyday life. If you leave marks, dust, or spatters in places they shouldn't be, then it's no better than living in a home full of clutter. An accumulation of dust is also just gross as hell, did you know most dust is made up entirely of skin cells? DEAD SKIN CELLS? That's disgusting, we don't need that shit in our homes!

Fun Exercise #31 - Scrubbing the "Hard to Reach" Areas

Below, make sure every area listed is COMPLETELY scrubbed because otherwise, you're living in some nasty shit! Dust, vacuum, sweep or blow out these areas if you can. If you have a pressure washer, you could even clean places like decks and porches. Again, don't worry about floors yet, we're just making sure any unusual places haven't been missed!!!

EXERCISE# 31
SCRUBBING THE "HARD TO REACH" AREAS

Date:-------

HARD places	Cleaned ✓
Ceiling fans and lights	☐
refrigerator	☐
above and under refrigerator	☐
under sink cabinets	☐
drawers	☐
book shelves	☐
book shelves	☐
Clear drains	☐
Stove	☐
Oven	☐
Above or Under Cabinets	☐
baseboards	☐

In case you're concerned that all your possessions that you've now taken time to organize won't be able to find their home, or will continue wandering around, let me take a moment to assuage that concern. Take a moment to look in the mirror and say aloud: "Naaahhh, stop worrying!" Because frankly, that's exactly how you should be feeling about your present circumstances. Thanks to all the crap you've already committed to getting rid of earlier, that means you should have a ton of space leftover to do exactly what you want to do with everything you have left. After all, at this point, there should be tons of open space to store your items. If there isn't, then what the hell? Get your ass back to the start of the book and do it all over again! You need to get rid of everything that you've proven to yourself you don't flipping need! At this point, there should be so much space that you can't even fill it all left.

Which could lead to another problem. "There's so much open space now, I just have to fill it up!" Get that mindset OUT OF HERE! So many people think that the moment there's one little bit of empty room, it means you have to fill it with something! Have you ever witnessed how some people, when they come in the front door after work, immediately set down their backpack, purse, or book bag onto an open table right by the front door and freaking leave it there? Maybe you've even done this yourself? Here's the tea: That's FREAKING ANNOYING. You might not think this behaviour is bad necessarily. Who doesn't wanna set their things down the moment they get home? Well, let me phrase it this way: Say, you're married. You spend all day cleaning your house using this book. Your dining room is right next to the front door. Now, you've just finished going through this whole book, and you're taking a step back to admire your work. Then suddenly your lovely partner comes in the door and stomps their muddy boots on the ground before throwing their coat and lunchbox or purse onto your freshly cleaned dining table. They then proceed to trek mud through your shared home, kicking off their boots as they do for you to pick up later, their socks, and then throw their laundry into the middle of the room you just cleaned up. They go to the shower, pulling out fifteen different objects as they do that, they leave on the shared bathroom sink.

Now your house is gross after hours upon hours of hard work to the contrary. You think you'd be pissed off? Imagine me when my own partner came in and felt the need to leave a trail of trash all around them as they came in! Yeah, I was freaking mad. So, if you'd be mad at someone coming in and mucking up your hard work instantly, shouldn't you then be mad at yourself for ever thinking about doing the same exact habits? Okay, so the term *thinking* about it isn't quite accurate. Rather, it's an unconscious habit we all do. We get home, we're tired, we fill the first empty spot we see with our belongings. That desire to fill empty parts of our home with our things is very common, but this is a habit you must break off of yourself and those in your household if you don't want your house looking like rats are living in it again.

Now that your house is decluttered and organized, look around. Is there more space that can be gained? Is there more you can do to ensure you don't resume your bad habit of putting things where they don't belong just because you're tired? By planning ahead, you'll save yourself time and energy you could spend doing other things you genuinely enjoy, rather than cleaning up after yourself or others.

Fun Exercise #32 - Planning Ahead for Being Mega Tired

Here's a fun little piece of trivia about me. One time, I was so exhausted from work that I left my keys in my doorknob, stripped on my way to the shower, bathed, then fell asleep. When I woke up again, it was five o'clock in the evening and I had no freaking clue where anything was. My keys were the worst of it, I looked everywhere and still couldn't figure out where I had left them! I was about to give up when I opened my door, and voila. In the very keyhole! Luckily, no creep came up and took them, but it also happened that my door was away from where anyone would be wandering. To prevent this from happening, or for that matter preventing yourself from filling ANY open space in your house with shit you don't need, you need to make a system. Now that you have places for everything, run drills. Practice going through the motions; if you're exhausted, where will you put your keys? Your clothes? Your paperwork? If you see a sale at IKEA, train yourself to say NO. You do NOT need that cheap-ass kitchen gadget to fill your shelf, so forget about it!

In this exercise, write about how you plan to stop yourself from giving in to temptation. What will you do to avoid filling in the empty spaces of your home with things? How will you show others in your household, and yourself, how to properly put things away even when you're exhausted?

EXERCISE# 32
PLANNING AHEAD FOR BEING MEGA TIRED

Date:------

Below, put some plans about what to do when tired, and how you'll stop yourself from making the same mistakes that got you to this point.

Plan A

Plan B

Plan C

Self Reflection 17

Do you recall a time where you were so blatantly exhausted that you couldn't keep yourself from passing out before you could do anything? In that situation, exactly what happened? What were the circumstances? Were there any consequences for that happening? How did it affect you or your relationships to those around you?

How About I Put It in Storage?

HOW ABOUT YOU DON'T? Sorry to say, but I am not at all a fan of storage systems, techniques, units, or any ideas regarding storing anything at all. The only exception I can really make would be for something like putting away holiday decorations, but even then, they shouldn't require their very own room. Why would you want a room full of garbage that you don't use? That's totally detrimental to everything you've tried to accomplish up until this moment! Furthermore, if you buy more shit to store things in, that just goes back to the precious problem: having more empty space to fill! Screw that, whatever you need right now should be more or less within an arm's reach! The whole concept of "saving it for later" when it comes to dining sets or pieces of furniture by shoving it into storage that you pay for on a monthly basis is a HUGE cardinal sin in the realm of decluttering!

Now, unless you are a bonafide redneck who keeps their Christmas lights up all year long (yeehaw!), you do still have the issue of the remaining items that are purely seasonal. Of course, I'm not a HEATHEN, I don't keep my Saint Patrick's Day clover decorations in my window next to my Easter egg decals and my Halloween pumpkins. In those cases, and a few others depending, some storage is acceptable. The keyword here is: simple. It's far too easy to fall into the Amazon Trap of buying the newest gadget guaranteed to make your storage into gold… or something along those lines. Here's the hard facts; no, you do not need a hundred-gallon large resin box to put things away in. No, you don't have anywhere to put those cute folding storage cubes. No, that ottoman with storage inside of it will not save you space because the fact it exists does not actually get rid of the problem because it is also taking up space in your house. No, that eight-cube, easy-to-assemble wire rack is not worth it because it breaks apart in a stiff breeze, so why does it say it's supposed to hold books or shoes—why would it freaking lie?! That last one I might have a bit of knowledge about from experience.

Due to the myriad of products we see, we so often think, "Oh, this would be perfect for putting my XYZ in back home!" Stop that. Spray yourself with water like you're a cat or some shit if you have to, but do NOT do that thing. That is a trap for your money, and a trap to build back up all that clutter you just got rid of! Even worse, by putting things away where you can't see them, you're more likely to forget you have them at all, which leads to buying even more crap. So, when it comes to having any storage at all, keep it simple. Dedicate a storage space to each member of your family, so even young kids can be responsible about it. Children I've worked with loved that they could have their own, small area to store things in and call their own. The challenge is making sure everything you have fits into the small storage space, which is key to your success in keeping down your clutter.

Fun Exercise #33 - Minimize Your Storage

When it comes to figuring out just how you're going to store things WITHOUT spending a bundle on fresh contraptions to make it happen, carefully choose to have no more storage bins in your house than you can count on one hand. (If you have six fingers on one hand, lucky you! If you have four fingers or fewer, just make your storage bin limit five or less!) If you haven't done so already, sort through your storage. Keep only extra linens, some seasonal decorations, and only three photo albums. If you have more photo albums than that, consolidate them as best you can, then put them on your bookshelf rather than keeping them in storage. As for anything else you find in storage, use your best judgment. Keep only what can fit into your limited number of storage bins, make sure you clearly label them on the outside, so you don't have to rummage through the exteriors, then put them away. As for the rest of the crap you find in these storage bins, you know the drill. Recycle, trash, donate, or sell!

EXERCISE# 33
MINIMIZING YOUR STORAGE

Date:------

Do a sudden audit visit to your storage areas and sort everyting out. After you finish your (trash, sell, donate or recycle) review, the rest will go to ONLY 5 or less bins, write down the content of each bin for easy reach in the future.

	Contents
Bin# 1	
Bin# 2	
Bin# 3	
Bin# 4	
Bin# 5	

A nice bonus to this exercise is that as you write down your findings and in what storage bin, they're in, you can always refer back to this book if you can't find a certain item in storage. Be sure to carefully catalogue what you put into each bin below to save yourself the trouble later. Indexing your items is super freaking helpful!

Just to reiterate a few things: use your best judgment when it comes to all this. It's one thing for me to tell you how you should organize your storage, but also, I don't have eyes in your house, that'd be really creepy if I did. Whether you have a studio apartment or live in a five-story castle, you still need to be able to work with what you have. Live in a way that is minimalist enough that you never lose items again, and just make sure that everything has its proper space so that if you do lose track of it, you know exactly where to find it.

Natural organizing is the idea of keeping everything in its proper area so you don't lose your shit trying to find your glasses for the fifth time in the row on the same day or digging around for the remote in your couch cushions again. Logically, you can determine how different objects can belong to certain areas in your home. Keep the remote with the television, spoons in the kitchen. The more you practice putting things away where they belong, the easier it'll become over time until it becomes second nature. Kind of like practicing maintaining your posture—and if you straightened up after reading that, good for you! You won't become an absolute pretzel in old age! If you're worried about maintenance, then don't be. Everything comes with time, and eventually maintaining your freshly decluttered home will become as easy as walking through your front door.

With all that said above, I believe that I'm about to deliver you some space-saving storage hacks that will rock your socks off your feet and straight into the laundry basket because you shouldn't throw those nasty things directly onto the floor!

Organizing Your Wardrobe

Yes, yes, I know we went through this all before, but when it comes to organizing your clothes, it's so much more than just getting rid of the pieces you're no longer interested in using or having. Anyone who owns pants, shorts, shirts, shoes, and accessories needs to know how to organize their closets and ensembles of clothing to maximize the utility of their wardrobes (unless you're a total nudist). To do this, there are a few different general techniques you can implement that will make your life easier. At least, it'll beat trying to maintain a mess every single day!

Fun Exercise #34 - Russian Nesting Bags!

This includes talking about wallets too, for you men out there! Ladies and Theydies, let's face it. It's difficult to find a proper way to store your bags. Well, unless you're a declutter wizard like me! What I've found works best for me is playing "Russian Nesting Dolls" with my bag collections! "What the heck does that mean?" I hear you ask. To explain, I'm referring to Matryoshkas, the Russian Nesting Dolls that fit into each other. You pop one open, and a smaller doll is inside! This continues until you get to an impossibly small-sized little doll that's as cute as a button, and possibly of the same scale. This is what I do with my bags!

EXERCISE# 34
RUSSIAN NESTING BAGS!

Date:------

Bag description	Type	Size	General use	How often you use it?

Now, I don't expect you or anyone to have the same exact bags in varying scale, unless you pay top dollar for some designer stuff, but that's fine. Just do what you choose the biggest bag or purse that you own, then organize by size, go from largest to smallest. By the end of creating your make-shift nesting doll, you'll have saved a TON of space by compacting it all down into one bag. It'll even be really easy to pick and choose which purse you want whenever because all you'll have to do is pull it straight out of the "nest" by its handles, and remove any purse that's inside of it. In the area below, draw each bag and label it with its general use, the type of bag it is (evening clutch, gym bag, etcetera), and how often you use it.

BONUS: Make it a habit to pull out all the contents of your purse or bag when you get home, leaving the essentials out where they can be ready to go for the next bag you need to use when necessary. This will really help you stay organized and follow the rule of keeping things where you know they're going to be. Just be careful not to forget about them when first starting out with this new aspect of your routine.

Self Reflection 18

Have you seen any cool storage hacks online that don't involve having to buy some new, exotic means of storage? If not, would you ever consider using some to make your life easier? Have you got any cool storage hacks you've made yourself? If not, do you think someone you know may have some you could use?

Let's talk a little bit more about your closet before we move on. Speaking about the amount of potential in the space you have in your closet, by now you should have a crapload of space to use! After all the shit you've gotten rid of, all the organizing you've done, it's looking fantastic. So, let's finish off working on it like a badass. You'll follow my method of sorting clothing out based on time of year and use, dedicating certain areas of the closet for one element of clothing, and other spaces for another element.

The top space of your closet should be dedicated to off-season clothing. So, if you're in summer, take your thick-ass parka and park it up top! If you're in winter, keep your skimpy, sexy bathing suit in that location. You'll be rotating this out as the year goes on so that it's in a cyclical nature for the seasons. All the more reason to have something to wear at any time of the year! The garments that you use daily, such as pajamas, loungewear, season-appropriate clothing, and so on should be in the middle area, where you'll be able to access them the easiest. Wherever your hands naturally go when you think of "middle" should be where you find your usual wear. This way you minimize time finding something to wear for the day. Everything should be in one nice area to prevent you from stooping, searching, or rummaging; the point of decluttering and organizing is to make your life easier, dammit. As for the bottom area, thanks to your use of the previous spaces, it is a good place to store electronics. Your laptop, cell phone, chargers, game stations, and so on can all be put here. Why at the bottom of the closet? Well, if your electronics fall from a low height, they're less likely to receive damage than if falling from, say, the top of your closet. This is also good for the sake of storage because keeping these electronics so close means they're easy to swipe up at a moment's notice when you need them.

By the Way!

When it comes to other elements of your wardrobe, pertaining specifically to shoes, scarves, hats, and other accessories, there are a few different things you should try. You should have sorted through the shoes to see what you needed to get rid of versus what to keep back in chapter three, but in case that wasn't a category you considered previously, do that now. Sort the shoes by trying each pair on, determining if you still like them or if they are still functional, if they're not then get rid of them with your preferred method of disposal for shoes. Store the shoes either on a shoe rack near the entrance to your home or in your closet where you can rotate them seasonally for the appropriate weather with the rest of your general clothing. Another idea is that you can keep them in the original shoebox they came in, with more than one pair per box. Keep the seasonal shoes together with seasonal clothing to maximize efficiency when deciding outfits in a way that you can see them right away.

When it comes to other accessories like hats, scarves, and so on will depend a little on what you have available to you. I do recommend storing lighter items, such as scarves or headbands, neatly folded in top drawers. Heavier items should go on the bottom drawers for the same reasons as electronics being stored on lower shelves: protecting the items by ensuring there's no risk of fall damage. Otherwise, items can be hung on hangers.

While deciding what items should go where—I cannot emphasize it enough. Seasonal, seasonal, seasonal. If you have a means to be able to rotate accessories with your outfits, possibly by planning out pairings for certain items (for example, what shirt to wear with what set of earrings, what scarf goes with what pair of pants or shoes, and so on). You can always use scratch paper to draw out outfit pairings as we did back in exercise #21, "C'mon, Vogue!" In fact, I highly recommend doing so for every article of clothing you have and think about how to pair them with the accessories and shoes you own. It's a great way to kill an afternoon, so be the bad bitch you know you are and do a little fashion show with either friends or for just yourself! It's a badass way to build confidence in a wardrobe you already own.

Fun Exercise #35 - A Scenario Game

Below are two scenarios I've created. Read both of them carefully and then answer the question at the end.

    1. Imagine you're headed out to spend some time at your local cafe with friends to work on a project in the middle of autumn. However, due to a faulty alarm, you're in serious danger of running late. You've done all the above steps mentioned about how to organize your closet, though. Thanks to this, you have all your seasonal outfits right in front of you. You swipe up a cute shirt, a perfect jacket, wrap a scarf around your neck, pull on some fashionable jeans and socks, put on your adorable boots, and don a hat. You would have forgotten your laptop and charger too if it wasn't right there in front of you in the closet! You select a bag from your Matryoshka nest that fits your style and size needed for your laptop, put in all the essentials including your laptop, keys, charger, cell phone, and wallet before you head out to the cafe in style. Thankfully, you've taken to putting your favourite sunglasses with your essentials every day too, so you can pull them on and look fresh out of the page of a magazine strutting into the cafe right on time. You have a blast with your friends, get work done, and sip the beverage of your choice.

    2. You're back to your life before getting this workbook. Same situation, you've woken up and are now in danger of being late to the cafe meeting. Scrambling, you dig through your clothing frantically for the fall weather but can only find your summer clothes because you forgot to swap everything out. You pull on a tank top and shorts along with a thin jacket. You snag your phone and laptop, shoving them into the first bag you see that fits the laptop, put on some shoes, and hurry out the door, locking it from the inside behind you. You make it to the cafe on time, but you're shivering the whole way as the

crisp autumn morning hits with its (usually) tantalizing wind. As you huddle up to your friends, you realize you forgot your charger and the laptop is dead. You think of warming up with a beverage, only to realize after you've made your order that you left your wallet at home. A friend pays for it for you, and you promise to pay them back for it when you can. After getting some work done, you head back home, shivering all the while, and go to open the door... only to realize you've locked yourself out because the keys are just inside the door.

This sounds like a dumb question, but which scenario would you prefer to live through? Have you experienced something like this before? What would you want to do if you got yourself into scenario two?

EXERCISE# 35
A SCENARIO GAME

Date:-----

Write down about your experience in a similar situation:

When in Doubt, You Don't Need It

For the final topic I want to touch on for this chapter, I want to make something crystal freakin' clear. If you see something in the store and you're considering taking it home: leave it the hell alone. Don't inspect it, don't get closer to look at the price, leave it the heck be. Ignore the giant "SALE!!" signs you see everywhere. The fact is, the only way you'll save money is if you don't spend it. There is no "saving money" by purchasing things proclaiming to be on sale, on clearance, or otherwise. That includes items that come in bulk, that shit may seem like a great deal, but it also has the added deficit of taking up space in your house. Again, do not be tempted to fill up your empty spaces with more stuff. It's empty because it's clean, the more you tell yourself this the easier it will be to say "no" to anything that may catch your eye. Before you know it, you'll have saved a ton of money by simply walking away from purchases that you frankly don't freaking need!

In other words, store stuff in the shop, not in your home! This saying was given to me when I was a child. Most parents encourage you to finish your plate when you eat, but not mine. They would say, "if you're not hungry, then store the food in the trash, not your stomach." As a result, I've thrown or given away food I wasn't going to eat to friends also eating with me, or family members in similar situations. By not consuming food I didn't need, I've managed to keep the weight off as well. Your body stores away the food you eat for later, which is how weight is gained. Apply that same idea to your home. When thinking of what to put in it, would adding yet another piece of furniture simply starts to make your house "overweight?"

Fun Exercise #36 - Training Your Willpower

Dare yourself. Go into a store that sells furniture, look around, and buy NOTHING. You heard me. NOTHING. Don't look at prices if you can help it, and don't buy a goddamned thing. Do, however, write down pieces you think are cute, where they could be placed in your house, how you would use it… then cross it out, and never think about it again. The only reason you should ever buy more crap is to replace things you already had.

EXERCISE# 36
TRAINING YOUR WILLPOWER

Date:-----

You know what to do after you fill out each line right?
CROSS IT OUT!

Cute item / potential buy	Description	Where to put? How to use?

Self Reflection 19

How do you feel now that your home is completely organized? Your house by now should be shining. Spotless, and clean as a whistle. Is the air fresher? Do you feel more relaxed? Are you shocked by how much empty space there is now? Record your feelings about your current state of living and how it has affected you so far.

CHAPTER FIVE: DECLUTTER YOUR LIFE!

Well, holy shit, you made it! In less than one year, you've gotten your shit completely together. By now, your house should be so immaculate that the pope would be willing to spit on it. Before you run to the local Catholic church to beg the pope to visit though (or whatever affiliation you have, if any at all), just hold the phone for a moment. You didn't get this far without making a few mistakes—that is, building up the mess in the first place is undoubtedly a monument to those exact issues. We touched on this in the first chapter, but now I'm bringing it back in full force: a cluttered space is a cluttered mind. The clutter of your space is gone now, but how is your mind? All throughout this workbook, I've dropped lots of places for you to write in your own thoughts about how things were going. This was either a pause in cleaning, a moment to just relax, or time to centre yourself. What the hell do you do to even make sure it never gets this bad again? What clutter is there left, outside of your home, that you can take care of? It doesn't stop at the edge of your doorway; it begins and ends with you.

There are a few different methods one could go about attempting to mitigate clutter for the rest of their life, but I'm only gonna focus on this element: what's inside your heart. Not to get all gross and mushy, but the fact is that if you feel unhappy, then your surroundings will reflect that. When a movie is being made, set dressers (if they're good, that is) will take the time to put together the bedroom of the main character. What does it say about them? Photos on the mirror, scented candles on the windowsill, a desk covered in books. It's all a snapshot of their reality, and it's what the creators of a film want you to know about that character. So, then, when you take a snapshot of your own reality, what do you see?

Do you have beer bottles on the coffee table next to a pack of cigarettes? Is your laundry neatly folded in your drawers or thrown in without care? What is the colour and pattern of your bedsheets? To be crystal clear; I'm not here to pass judgments. I'm asking you to judge them yourself. Think deeper about what your surroundings mean about you, at least in the elements that you can control. What conditions does someone live in that showcase that they are unhappy? What conditions does someone live in to show that they are successful? There is a certain truth to the power of attraction in the sense of personal paths. If you surround yourself with things that reflect your desires, then eventually those things will give you the leg up you need to pursue them.

Without getting super deep into a bunch of bullshit crystal magic, blah-blah, it's the same idea of the saying, "dress for the job you want." If you want to invite filth into your life, then live in filth. If you want your life to be simpler, then live minimalistically. If you want to live a life pretending to be a millionaire when you're actually living hand-to-mouth, then live in poverty. Okay, that last one might have been a bit mean-spirited, but you get the idea. Dress for the job you want equates also to live the way you want your life to be.

In other words, unless you want this sort of thing for some reason, don't collect shit you don't need, don't invite people into your home you don't trust, and don't allow yourself to be stuck in the past by surrounding yourself with nostalgic memorabilia. There's so much life you can live when you're free of the unnecessary burdens that come with a messy home, and with this book, you've gotten so much closer to it. The last part, though, comes within you and who or what surrounds you.

Declutter Your Social Circles

Do you genuinely know who has your back and who doesn't? By allowing people who are constantly negative into our lives, we allow our minds to make room and engage in behaviour that is detrimental to ourselves above all else. This person could be a fake friend whose only intent is to constantly one-up you in every situation, making a competition out of every petty element of your life, or in general is just unpleasant. They could also be a jerk of a romantic ex-partner, which can be especially dangerous at times; use your best judgment while getting away from this individual and make sure they absolutely cannot reach you because there can be times when their presence in your life is also dangerous. This also goes for a toxic relative, though it may be more difficult to cut them out of your life, there's plenty of ways to minimize exposure however you can. The truth is it's easier now than ever to make new friends and find fresh faces. For the technologically savvy, try joining a Facebook or online blog group catered to your interests. Go to meetups, say hello to the cashier at your local supermarket. Or, if you prefer a more intimate approach, try looking into an event happening near you and make an effort to speak to someone there. It could even be your local senior centre, you'd be amazed at the incredible shit old people have to say, and I mean that seriously. Old folks are generally happy to have company, consider it your good deed for the day, week, month, etcetera.

Decluttering your social circles means throwing the phony friends in the trash where they belong in a respectful way. Be the bigger man by not responding to a mean text or ignoring them at a party when they try to approach you. Those assholes look only to feed on your energy, so don't give them any. Out with the old and in with the new; In other words, find some better friends that genuinely enjoy your company and support you, not ones that make you feel like crap all the time!

Fun Exercise #37 - Blocked, Blocked, Blocked!

When it comes to dealing with crappy people, especially online, there's an amazing feature on almost all websites. Blocking! I love blocking people that are annoying! I challenge you, right now, to block all the toxic people in your life on social media (or mute them, if blocking would cause stupid drama). In real life, there's almost an equally good way of dealing with shitty people, it's called ignoring! Now, that's what I call a life hack! Try it, you might just like it. Below, write down who you're "blocking" for good and why!

EXERCISE# 37
BLOCKED, BLOCKED, BLOCKED!

Date:------

I blocked/ muted/ ignored	Because

Decluttering Your Work

This one might be a bit tricky due to the numerous facets that come with it. First, you could work in a myriad of different places that all have different levels of being clean and how much you can control that. Second, you could even work from home and happen to clean your workspace while doing this book. If so, then the only thing you should worry about is getting rid of connections to any toxic co-workers or supervisors you have.

For the sake of example, let's just say you work in an office for now. When was the last time you cleaned out your desk? Wiped down your keyboard with disinfectant? Sprayed it out with a can of aerosol? Dusted the area? Of course, you don't have to work in an office to make this work. Wipe down your general work area with a good disinfectant and give it a good scrub overall. Sort through your personal drawers like at a desk, or a work locker. Make sure there isn't something there that you've left behind by mistake, you may surprise yourself!

Lastly but most importantly, your co-workers or supervisors. You may be able to get away from fake friends or crappy family members, but you're literally paid to work beside awful people sometimes. There's no good ultimate means for getting away from this, but for that, all I can say is keep your attitude as clean as you can. If someone is nasty to you, be professional in your responses to them. Don't let anyone ruffle your feathers no matter how hard they try, and eventually, they'll give up. If you do experience any harassment though, report it to the proper person. There comes a time where workplace drama is more than just drama: it's a distraction from your ability to perform. You make sure that shit doesn't stand between you and your bread money!

Fun Exercise #38 - Stay Classy

First of all, where the hell do you work? How are you gonna clean up your workstation? Lastly, is anyone bothering you at work? Make a game plan now on how to deal with them the next time some stupid bullshit on their part comes up again. Aim to be professional, keep it classy, and take matters into your own hands if push comes to shove. Remember what they would tell you in grade school: Start by walking away, then tell them to stop, THEN get someone to help!

EXERCISE# 38
STAY CLASSY

Date:-----

Write down your thoughts about cleaning up and organizing your workspace, including how you plan to deal with your crappy co-workers!

Self Reflection 20

Who are the people who have made your life, in some way or another, worse? When did you meet them? What was your story in regards to them? What are you going to do to make sure they don't ever harm you again or bring down your bad-bitch self? These people are clutter: trash to be thrown away. Good riddance without them!

Declutter Your Decisions

With so many other aspects of your daily life now straightened and decluttered in many different ways, now we can go to the true source of any clutter that gathers: your heart and mind. When it comes to your heart, consider any turmoil you have and find a means to relieve it. This could mean speaking to a therapist, which I always highly recommend, or something as simple as keeping a daily journal to record your thoughts. As for your mind, if you find yourself often stuck between a rock and a hard place for choosing between factors beyond your control, weigh your options carefully. There is harm in stagnancy and waiting too long to make any decision could mean you lose an opportunity altogether. With a better, less cluttered home to think in now though, you may just find it's easier than ever to make up your mind on things that may have left you paralyzed before. Try not to pressure yourself, because frankly, that's just a whole other kind of clutter you don't need.

To make good decisions, you need a decluttered mind. Many of my friends and family who have applied these methods in this book throughout their life have proven to me time and time again how effective it is. By starting with the place, you spend most of your time, your home, and working your way up from there, you've begun to understand the importance of just what it means to live a life free of clutter. Those that I've personally helped organize their homes have been able to make huge, life-altering decisions once they had the space to work in. They would always tell me that, due to how they were stuck inside their houses or apartments with all the things and stuff they thought they needed, those possessions legitimately held them back. After reducing everything down to only what they really wanted, really needed, loved, related to their interests, hobbies, and passions, they could begin to work on themselves as people. Some of my friends have even quit the jobs they hated, instead starting businesses in the fields they were most interested in or getting a job in them.

When it comes to changing your life, seeing things differently is key. It's so easy to become a nasty little hermit crab, so content inside in our little shells away from the world until we see some other shell we like better. The grass isn't greener on the other side, though, it's perfect right within your own space—provided you make it that way first. When you make your world brighter by getting rid of all the crap that blocks the things that are most important, your sense of judgment becomes better too. With your home now in a totally zenned-out state of minimalism, you'll be able to breathe, think, and live again.

Fun Exercise #39 - Time Travel

Now go back to that time before the great un-fuckening of your life (that is, you are getting through this book) and recall the mess you lived in. What was it like? Did it ever ruin an event for you or make you feel like crap? How do you feel now that your house is no longer like that? Talk to a great extent about all this, because frankly, you deserve to remember why you can NEVER go back to that shit!!

EXERCISE# 39
TIME TRAVEL

Date:-----

Write down your recount of the situation you had before using this book:

Why Can't I Just Let Stuff Go?

At the end of the day, you're going to be letting go of a lot of stuff while using this book. If you haven't thrown ANYTHING away at all, it may mean a more significant problem is present that you should seek help with therapy—that's way the hell out of my realm of expertise. I've said it over and over again throughout these pages, the simplest way to make a decision about what to trash, sell, recycle or donate is to question yourself. You can hold it, touch it, and feel its connection to you depending on whatever item you have trouble getting rid of. Ask yourself these two questions, the first one being "Do I need it now or in the future?" The second question you need to ask yourself is, "Do I really love or admire this object?" If the answer is no to either question, then it's clutter. Tell yourself that, repeat it aloud if you need to. "It's clutter, it's clutter, it's clutter." Once you sever your mental or emotional connection to, let's face it, basic crap you could probably replace in a heartbeat, throwing away the items becomes that much easier.

To have difficulty throwing certain items away is completely human. The hardship for this issue stems mostly from having memories, either good or bad, that make us feel like we HAVE to hold onto shit that's literally bad for us. However, continuing to hold onto these objects holds a massive freaking rain cloud over us, one that blocks out the sunshine of a new day. If you look at old objects you have and think, "I can't get rid of this, my friend gave it to me!" or, "my mom will be so disappointed that I didn't end up using it—"so what? It was sentimental the moment you got it, but it's served its purpose now. It made you feel better for a time, but when was the last time you truly even remembered you had it? Over time, the things we think of as important to us lose their initial punch of love, ultimately becoming a useless waste of space. Literal, physical space that you need to grow. So chuck that shit out, take a deep breath, and push forward, you fine ass bitch.

If the item in question isn't so much sentimental as it is potentially useful, ask yourself what for? Is your thought not so much, "I got this from my cousin's friend's great-grandma," but more along the lines of, "but I might need this soon!" Then, have you needed it in a year? For an item that may be effective, such as an article of clothing, a tool, workout equipment (yes, this is a callout), or an old laptop, they must be functional. These are sometimes questionable, especially if you've had them for a long time. When it comes to this item and your thoughts of, "but I might need this soon," then when did you use it *last?* It's one thing to have a set of special dishes that you use once around the holidays because you use them at least once a year for a special occasion, it's another to have some rusty bag of tools lying around that you haven't used in ages. Throw it out and replace your gear with fresh ones whenever you find you need them unless you're looking to get tetanus disease in the near future. This idea applies to all the crap that has practical use. Right now, from the date you're reading this, when did you last use it? If it was over a year ago (or several,) chuck that shit out! It served its purpose at one point (or didn't come out of the packaging at all), so clearly you no longer need it now. Don't worry though, if in the future you need this certain item you could always either buy a new one or ask to borrow one from a friend or family member depending on what it is.

Fun Exercise #40 - Seriously, Just Let It Go!

No more sweet talking! If you haven't already, list out these items that are hard to get rid of for you. Write down WHY you think you should keep it, and then write down WHY you think it should go. Have you used it whatsoever in the past year as of this date? Also, do you have any items that you keep around for use only once a year, like special dishes for holiday meals? If so, don't worry about it! Just write out how you use them so you can justify keeping them. That's the rule, if you can justify it to yourself, it's yours! If not, it's gotta go right in the freaking trash!

EXERCISE# 40
SERIOUSLY, JUST LET IT GO!

Date:-----

'Hard to get rid of' item	Why should you keep it?	Why you shouldn't?	Last time used?	Plan to get rid of it (Trash, donate, sell etc.)

Self Reflection 21

This part can be really hard for some. What sentimental item have you had to get rid of before? What one are you getting rid of now, if any? Do you have concerns about throwing out a potentially useful item, and if so why? What can you do to mitigate those concerns? Is there a way for you to take time to relax to ease the stresses of any of this?

Finding the Pattern

Now that you're through it all, it's the perfect time to sit back and look at all the work you've done. What similarities have you picked up on throughout your time working through this book on all the items you had? If you had a collection, then it's easy to say you like collecting things resembling that item. In essence, you should be evaluating things you've purchased to see if there's anything about them that could tell you more about yourself and your habits. Your personality, your passions, your interests, and everything that makes you happy should be called into question. Frankly, you need to knock that shit off. You don't need twenty different versions of the same item, but you can use this information to your advantage. Using what you know about the things you had, you'll be able to make better decisions in the future.

Let's say for example that you realized you like the things you own to have a floral pattern on them. As a result, your dishes, drinkware, accessories, electronics, and everything else all had flowers on them. However, collecting these items by purchasing them isn't really sustainable for your brand-new decluttered lifestyle. You're trying to cut down on clutter, after all. Instead of reaching for yet another overpriced flowery accessory, you can evaluate that what you really like is flowers. This is honestly a perfect excuse to take up a new hobby. Figure out what you can and can't have in your house based on space, do your research, get a few flowerpots, and maintain flowers in your home or just outside of it with a brand-new garden. That's just one idea of how you could incorporate your hobbies or the things you like from items you no longer have or tend to accumulate: just going into them hog wild. Not all interests lead to being able to reasonably pick up gardening, but the thought is still there. Like model trains? Take a further interest by field-tripping to a few train stations. Like ants? Get an ant farm and dedicate an area to them. Enjoy yoga or going to the gym? Go to yoga classes, a lot of studios have mats and items you can use there, also the gym has all the workout equipment you could probably dream of. Breaking down the message of this, there are alternatives to storing a bunch of crap in your house when you can honestly minimize it or go to outside sources for it. Alternatively, go all-in with your house theme to surround yourself with the things you like, as mentioned previously. Plan to have a home that revolves around your likes and interests, just don't give in to the clutter-bug, dammit!

When you're able to identify exactly where your problem begins, what sets off your need to grab any old crap off the shelf, you can prevent it in the future. It's like the old saying goes, an ounce of prevention is worth a pound of cure. By being able to control your impulses, you'll not have to go through this whole book again the next time the shit starts to pile up. Go for alternatives that feed those interests of yours outside of dragging things home.

Fun Exercise #41 - Finding the Pattern

What is your specific hobby? How has it taken up room in your home? Below, list all the objects that have similarities in your home. This could be a certain colour, pattern, or concept. At the end, try to come to a conclusion about what these items mean, how they've affected you in your building of the clutter, and what you can do to consciously prevent yourself from picking up a multitude of these items again.

EXERCISE# 41
FINDING THE PATTERN

Date:------

List down objects that have similarities in your home. This could be a certain hobby stuff, color, pattern, or concept:

Conclusion:

Living Digital

Hold it! Before you roll your freaking eyes at the title of this section, be patient for a second, will you?! I know some of us aren't as tech-savvy as the others, but it doesn't matter. The fact is that by using technology to our advantage, we can minimize the build-up of shit we don't need by leaps and bounds! This can be anything from storing photos of items you were afraid to get rid of, keeping your money in a bank where you can access it electronically, and keeping all your paperwork digital where it's safe. This way you save paper, and thus save trees! Don't you want to be an economically savvy person?! Yeah, you do! Circling back to this with banks, a lot of institutions or official organizations have a "go green" option you can use to receive all notifications via notification and email aside from getting notices in the mail. I love this option, not only are you using less natural resources, but you get your information faster and easier. This goes for almost anything you can think of! These days, we have the luxury of having the crap we usually store "just in case" like warranty paperwork, installation processes, how-to guides, appliance specs, and operation manuals available to us anytime online. Even IKEA, perhaps the world's best generator of shit you don't need, has their instruction manuals online on their website, free to use and download anytime you want. So, why even bother with keeping all the papers that could come with them?! After a while of saving these "important documents," they pile up and just add to the clutter you don't need! If you haven't thrown away any of those things I just listed, do it. Just look up the items you have instruction manuals or warranty info for, make sure you can get your digital copies, save them somewhere you won't lose them on your computer, and presto! A whole lot of shit you have lying around has yet another reason to go straight into the garbage bin!

BONUS TIP: Here's a hack I discovered when I was low on money at one point. I was keeping a friend company while they were shopping, and I spotted something that I felt I HAD to have.

However, with my low resources, there was little I could do to actually obtain it. At that time, I took a photo of what I wanted in addition to the price tag. As time went on, I originally planned to purchase it when I had the money. However, after a month, I looked at the photo again and I realized I really didn't need it. Try using this! The next time you're shopping, and you see something you want, take a photo of it with your phone! This way you'll be able to still look at it and satisfy that carnal "I need this now" part of your brain. If you still want it in a few months, go for it! That being said, you'll be surprised how often you'll decide against needing or wanting the item in question.

Fun Exercise #42 - Go Paperless!

Let's minimize the clutter by the maximum by doing the following:

    1. Scanning all important documents and backing them up onto your computer. Aside from essential things you absolutely need copies of, now you can easily access all your paperwork with a few clicks of a button! (If you don't have a scanner in your home, go to an office supply store and ask them to scan your paperwork and save it to a USB drive for you on request. You supply the USB drive, and they will likely charge a small fee for the service!)

    2. Go online to your bank or other organizations you're a part of and sign up to go paperless with all future correspondence. This has only one deficit in that you will start receiving a lot of email notifications. Be sure to sort through your email as you can to ensure nothing gets lost in the crowd, so to speak.

While you work on going paperless, try to record which institutions you're going paperless with here, and keep tabs on what documents you plan to scan and where you put them. Thanks to your now badass method of making sure everything stays in one place at a time, you'll be able to find out exactly where everything is on your computer and in your home.

EXERCISE# 42
GO PAPERLESS!

GO PAPERLESS

A GREEN planet IS A CLEAN PLANET

Date:--------

Scanned items	Where? (USB, cloud etc.)	List Institutions to go paperless with

Can I Lose Weight by Decluttering My House?

The quick and dirty answer to that is "yes and no." There are no scientific studies regarding if there is a connection between the two, after all, correlation is not causation. Speaking from experience, however, both myself, my friends, and my family all experienced a little weight loss through the actions of cleaning and maintaining our clean homes. By removing the heavy burden on our shoulders of living a life free of clutter, the air felt lighter, more energized than it had been before. I'm sure there's something about feng shui or other bullshit expressing exactly these sentiments, but I can only speak from what myself and others have gone through. The energy in your house becomes stagnant when it's harder to move through, like wading through molasses. All the motion and energy that's brought into the home when making a conscious effort to improve the area, in this case via decluttering, has spruced up the place! Now there's joy in the air, hope, and a whole lot of determination! When I saw others after they've gone through this project, I could just see it on their faces how much healthier they felt.

Say you're a practical person and you don't really believe someone's mood and energy could be so moved by their environment. In that case, I do have a practical hypothesis. When you live in an area full of clutter, there's less space, more dirt where you can't see it, more dust, less room to move around in, and the quality of your air decreases significantly due to all of the contributing factors. It's not easy to dust away all the dead skin cells and dust mites if you have a whole open cabinet full of tchotchkes! Thus, the opposite is also true if you live in an environment with a lack of clutter. Simple, basic shit, right?!

Decluttering your home has the added benefit of getting you moving. With all that physical activity while throwing away the crap you don't need in addition to the amount of bending, stooping, reaching, pulling, and so on, that you do with sorting, your blood circulation starts improving. Your heart loves this, as it's extremely good for you to get moving in a way that isn't so exhausting it drains you, but instead gets you going. You're so busy concentrating on the task in front of you, though, that you might not even think of it as exercise. That's just another reason why I love decluttering! It's simple, it's effective, and really anyone can do it.

This isn't necessarily true for everyone, but I know for me in this situation I happened to lose quite a bit of weight. As much as I hate to admit it, living in all the clutter was detrimental to my mental health, which reflected poorly on my body. Instead of putting in the effort to make myself a meal, I'd let my mountain of dishes stew in their juices in the sink and opt instead for takeout. As delicious as takeout is, it really didn't help me feel any better nor did it help keep off any of the calories contributing to my weight. Once I set my mind to finally getting all the crap I didn't need out of my house and taking care of my kitchen with it, I made up my mind to eat healthier too. Now instead of letting all the food I had bought go to waste in the fridge, I could eat it without guilt because I knew I would clean up the mess right away. After an extended time off of takeout and cooking food for myself, I'm happy to say that I lost at least fifteen pounds and kept it off for good.

My friends experienced something similar with varying degrees of success, and my family was in that same boat. I feel like if you get stuck on the take-out train, it's hard to get off if you're living in a cluttered home. It's just another reason to commit yourself to this lifestyle, as it improves your mind, your heart, and your body all at once. Who the hell could even ask for more?

Self Reflection 22

This is the final time in this book you will be able to record what you think. You've come so far, and now you're almost ready to set off. I have a few more words I'd like to share with you before you go. How do you feel now that it's almost over?